quick & easy

microwave cooking for one

catherine atkinson

based on an original book by Rena Croft

foulsham

LONDON • NEW YORK • TORONTO • SYDNEY

foulsham

The Publishing House, Bennets Close, Cippenham,
Berkshire, SL1 5AP, England

ISBN 0-572-02726-5

Copyright © 2001 W. Foulsham & Co. Ltd

Cover photograph by Peter Howard Smith

Printed in Great Britain by Cox & Wyman Ltd, Reading, Berkshire

Contents

Introduction

Whether you live alone or are simply having a solitary night in, cooking for one can be a chore and it's all too easy to settle for a chilled ready-meal out of a packet, or to take a trip to the takeaway.

Many people use their microwave just for reheating and defrosting, which is a pity as its potential is far greater: having a microwave enables you to enjoy fresh food fast. Undeniably, speed is one of the main advantages, but the microwave is also renowned for its ability to cook foods such as fish and vegetables to perfection and to make sensationally smooth sauces without a saucepan in sight. Other bonuses are that you needn't worry about forgetting food as the microwave always turns itself off, and it cooks with the minimum mess so you're not left with piles of washing up.

The recipes in this book are designed for one, so you don't have to divide the quantities in an ordinary cookbook to make a single portion. The ingredients are selected to use a range of meats and vegetables in cuts and quantities that are easy to buy on a small scale. If you do want to cook for more than one, simply multiply the quantities. If you double the quantity, increase the cooking times by about half as much again and check the food regularly until it is cooked to your liking.

You'll find everything you need here to get cooking: plenty of mouthwatering dishes to suit every occasion, from speedy and stylish snacks to midweek meals in moments and delectable double-quick desserts. So come on, spoil yourself – solo eating has never been so much fun!

Microwave Mastery

Read your manual carefully to find out exactly how your model works, then follow these top ten tips:

1 Use individual-sized cookware suitable for both cooking and serving to save washing up. The more regular the shape of the container the better: a round dish is preferable to an oval one, and a large shallow dish is better than a small, deep one.

2 Make sure that you always use microwave-proof cookware. Glass, pottery and china are all suitable, but avoid any dishes that contain metal. Don't use melamine or plastic when cooking foods with a lot of fat or sugar, as the heat of the food may make them melt.

3 Foods of a similar size should be arranged in a ring pattern for even cooking. Irregular-shaped foods such as chicken drumsticks should be positioned with the thickest part towards the outer edge of the dish.

4 Rotate food regularly by stirring, turning over or rearranging, especially if your microwave doesn't have a turntable.

5 Prick foods covered with a membrane or tight skin, such as jacket potatoes and egg yolks before cooking or they may burst.

6 Cook food uncovered unless otherwise stated. When covering, use pierced microwave-safe clingfilm (plastic wrap), or use a lid or plate.

7 Cover areas of food that are likely to overcook, such as the tail end of a whole fish, with small pieces of foil secured with wooden cocktail sticks (toothpicks), but make sure it doesn't touch the walls.

8 When you remove food from the microwave it retains heat and continues cooking, so many recipes allow time for the food to stand. This allows the heat to distribute evenly and completes cooking.

9 Wipe up spills when they occur: if you don't, they will absorb the microwave energy and may slow down the cooking time.

10 Keep safety in mind when removing food from the microwave: use oven gloves as dishes get very hot; always stir carefully and away from your face, as hot, dense liquids sometimes bubble up when stirred.

The Liberated Larder

Variety is a great boredom-beater and the key lies in keeping a well-stocked storecupboard. This can be difficult when you're cooking for one, as you don't want to buy in bulk and end up throwing away out-of-date foods. Build up the basics and you'll be able to return home late and produce a delicious dinner in minutes.

What's in Store?

Dried foods: Flour (buy in small bags), pasta, rice, bulghar (cracked wheat), couscous, dried fruits such as apricots and sultanas (golden raisins), nuts, creamed coconut powder.

Herbs, spices and seasonings: Bay leaves, chilli powder, ground cinnamon, ground coriander (cilantro), ground cumin, dried mixed herbs, salt and pepper, stock cubes or powdered stock (easier to mix up small quantities). Store spices in a cool dark place and buy in small quantities as they soon lose their pungency.

Oils: Olive, sunflower and sesame.

Jars, bottles and cartons: Mustard, pesto, lemon or lime juice, vinegars, soy sauce, ketchup (catsup), clear honey, peanut butter, long-life milk.

Cans: Chopped tomatoes, pulses such as kidney beans.

Fridge: Butter or margarine (suitable for cooking), tomato purée (paste), jars of ready-grated ginger and garlic (if used frequently), Cheddar, Parmesan and Mascarpone cheeses; crème fraîche, yoghurt, eggs, spring onions (scallions), shallots, fresh herbs such as parsley and coriander (cilantro).

Freezer: Breadcrumbs, peas, sweetcorn (corn), spinach, leftover chopped herbs, lean minced (ground) meat, chicken breasts, fish cuts such as salmon steaks, prawns (shrimp), pitta and naan breads.

Notes on the Recipes

✳ Do not mix metric, imperial and American measures. Follow one set only.

✳ All spoon measures are level: 1 tsp = 5 ml;
1 tbsp = 15 ml.

✳ Always wash, peel, core and seed, if necessary, fresh produce before use.

✳ Eggs are medium unless otherwise stated.

✳ The use of strongly flavoured ingredients such as garlic, chilli and ginger depends on personal taste and quantities can be adjusted accordingly.

✳ All the recipes serve one unless otherwise specified.

✳ Times are based on an 800-watt microwave oven. Cooking times in a microwave vary depending on the temperature of the food when cooking starts and the size and shape of the container. Always undercook initially rather than overcook and test the food regularly during cooking.

✳ If you have a microwave with a different wattage, adjust the cooking times as follows:

900 watts – subtract 10 seconds per minute
850 watts – subtract 5 seconds per minute
800 watts – no change
750 watts – add 5 seconds per minute
700 watts – add 10 seconds per minute
650 watts – add 15 seconds per minute
600 watts – add 20 seconds per minute.

✳ Different makes of microwave ovens have different settings: High refers to 100 per cent/full power output of 800 Watts; Medium to 60 per cent of full power; Low to 35 per cent of full power.

✳ The microwave used in creating these recipes had a turntable: if yours does not, it's important to turn and rotate food regularly during cooking.

✳ Preparation times given include both preparation and cooking and are approximate.

Soups

There's nothing quite as satisfying as a delicious soup made with fresh, seasonal ingredients. When cooking the conventional way, the hungry eater needs patience as the soup gently bubbles on the hob, but with a microwave you can enjoy home-made soup in little more time than it takes to open a can, knowing that much of the fresh flavour and nutrients has been retained.

The secret of a successful soup is a well-flavoured stock. If you haven't the time – or the inclination – to make your own, you can buy small cartons of fresh stock in the supermarket. Otherwise, use good-quality stock cubes or bouillon powder.

Minestrone with Pesto

15 g/½ oz/1 tbsp butter or margarine
5 ml/1 tsp olive oil
½ small onion, finely chopped
1 small carrot, chopped
½ celery stick, chopped
50 g/2 oz potato, peeled and cut into 1 cm/½ in dice
200 ml/7 fl oz/scant 1 cup boiling vegetable stock
200 g/7 oz/1 small can of chopped tomatoes
15 g/½ oz tiny pasta shapes
15 g/½ oz frozen peas, thawed
Salt and freshly ground black pepper
10 ml/2 tsp pesto
30 ml/2 tbsp freshly grated Parmesan cheese

1   Put the butter or margarine, oil and onion in a bowl. Stir, then microwave on High for 1 minute. Stir in the carrot, celery and potato and microwave on High for 3 minutes.

2   Stir in the stock, tomatoes and pasta. Cook, uncovered, on High for 6 minutes or until the vegetables and pasta are just tender.

3   Add the peas and season to taste with salt and pepper. Cook on High for 1 minute. Cover and leave to stand for 1 minute.

4   Transfer the soup to a serving bowl, drizzle the pesto over and sprinkle with the Parmesan before serving.

🕐 15 minutes

Cream of Mushroom Soup with Bacon

15 g/½ oz/1 tbsp butter or margarine
1 shallot, finely chopped
50 g/2 oz mushrooms, sliced
10 ml/2 tsp plain (all-purpose) flour
120 ml/4 fl oz/½ cup milk
120 ml/4 fl oz/½ cup vegetable stock
1 streaky bacon rasher (slice), rinded
15 ml/1 tbsp dry sherry (optional)
15 ml/1 tbsp crème fraîche or double (heavy) cream
15 ml/1 tbsp chopped fresh parsley
Salt and freshly ground black pepper

1   Place the butter or margarine, shallot and mushrooms in a bowl and microwave on High for 2–3 minutes until soft, stirring after 1 minute to coat.

2   Blend the flour with a little of the milk to make a smooth paste. Gradually stir in the remaining milk and the stock. Add to the mushrooms and microwave on High for 3 minutes, stirring once during cooking.

3   Purée the soup in a food processor or blender until smooth.

4   Put the bacon on a plate and cover with kitchen paper (paper towel). Microwave on High for 1½ minutes until crisp. Allow to cool slightly, then crumble.

5   Stir the sherry into the soup, if using, followed by the crème fraîche or cream and the parsley. Season to taste with salt and pepper and microwave on High for 30 seconds to reheat. Serve sprinkled with the bacon.

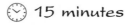 15 minutes

Asparagus Soup

15 g/½ oz/1 tbsp butter or margarine
100 g/4 oz asparagus, cut into chunks
50 g/2 oz potato, peeled and cut into 1 cm/½ in dice
2 spring onions (scallions), chopped
120 ml/4 fl oz/½ cup vegetable stock
120 ml/4 fl oz/½ cup milk
Salt and freshly ground black pepper
10 ml/2 tsp chopped fresh chervil or snipped fresh chives
15 ml/1 tbsp crème fraîche

1 Put the butter or margarine, asparagus, potato and spring onions in a large bowl. Cover and microwave on High for 4 minutes, stirring after 1 minute to coat.

2 Stir in the stock and milk. Season with salt and pepper, cover and microwave on High for 3–4 minutes, stirring once, until the vegetables are tender.

3 Purée the soup in a blender or food processor. Pour into a large soup bowl and microwave on High for 30 seconds or until piping hot. Stir in the chervil or chives and top with the crème fraîche before serving.

🕐 15 minutes

Fresh Salmon Soup

15 g/½ oz/1 tbsp butter or margarine
3 spring onions (scallions), sliced
10 ml/2 tsp plain (all-purpose) flour
150 ml/¼ pt/⅔ cup milk
2.5 ml/½ tsp Dijon mustard
100 g/4 oz skinned fresh salmon, cut into 2 cm/¾ in chunks
10 ml/2 tsp chopped fresh tarragon or dill (dill weed)
Salt and freshly ground black pepper

1   Put the butter or margarine and spring onions in a bowl, cover and microwave on High for 1 minute until soft.

2   Stir in the flour, then gradually blend in the milk. Stir in the mustard. Microwave, uncovered, on Medium for 3 minutes until the mixture thickens and bubbles, whisking halfway through cooking.

3   Stir in the salmon and microwave on Medium for 2½ minutes or until just cooked. Stir in the tarragon or dill and season to taste with salt and pepper. Leave to stand for 1 minute before serving.

⊘ 15 minutes

Chunky Vegetable and Bean Soup

15 ml/1 tbsp olive oil
½ celery stick, chopped
1 baby leek, cut into 1 cm/½ in slices
1 small carrot, halved and sliced
100 g/4 oz potato, diced
1 small garlic clove, crushed
200 g/7 oz/1 small can of chopped tomatoes
120 ml/4 fl oz/½ cup boiling vegetable stock
1 bay leaf
75 g/3 oz canned borlotti or cannellini beans, drained
15 ml/1 tbsp chopped fresh parsley
Salt and freshly ground black pepper

1 Put the oil in a bowl with the celery, leek, carrot, potato and garlic. Stir to coat, then microwave on High for 3 minutes, stirring halfway through cooking.

2 Stir in the tomatoes, stock and bay leaf. Cover and microwave on Medium for 10 minutes or until the vegetables are tender, stirring halfway through cooking.

3 Add the beans and parsley and salt and pepper to taste. Cover and cook on High for 1 minute. Leave to stand for 2–3 minutes before serving.

🕐 20 minutes

Vichyssoise

15 g/½ oz/1 tbsp butter or margarine
100 g/4 oz potato, peeled and diced
100 g/4 oz leeks, sliced
120 ml/4 fl oz/½ cup vegetable stock
100 ml/3½ fl oz/scant ½ cup milk
Salt and freshly ground black pepper
15 ml/1 tbsp double (heavy) cream or crème fraîche
10 ml/2 tsp snipped fresh chives

1 Put the butter or margarine, potato and leeks in a bowl with 45 ml/3 tbsp of the stock. Cover and microwave on High for 5 minutes, stirring once.

2 Add the remaining stock, cover and microwave on High for 4 minutes or until the vegetables are very tender. Stir in the milk, then purée in a blender or food processor until smooth.

3 Return the soup to the bowl and season generously with salt and pepper. Microwave on High for 3 minutes until bubbling.

4 Serve the soup topped with a swirl of cream or crème fraîche and sprinkled with the chives.

⊙ 20 minutes

✴ This soup is delicious served hot, but is equally good and more usually eaten chilled. Allow to cool after step 3, then cover and chill in the fridge for up to 24 hours. You may have to stir in a little more milk to thin the consistency before topping with the cream or crème fraîche and chives.

Rich Onion Soup

15 g/½ oz/1 tbsp butter or margarine
1 small onion, finely sliced
2.5 ml/½ tsp plain (all-purpose) flour
150 ml/¼ pt/⅔ cup good beef stock or canned consommé
Freshly ground black pepper
10 ml/2 tsp brandy (optional)
2 slices of French bread, toasted
25 g/1 oz/¼ cup Gruyère cheese, grated

1 Place the butter or margarine and onion in a bowl and microwave on High for 2½ minutes until soft, stirring once during cooking.

2 Stir in the flour, then blend in the stock or consommé and season with pepper. Microwave on High for 4 minutes, whisking twice during cooking. Stir in the brandy, if using, then cover the soup and leave to stand for 2 minutes.

3 Meanwhile, put the toast on a plate, sprinkle with the cheese and microwave on High for 30 seconds until the cheese has started to melt.

4 Serve the soup in a wide soup bowl with the cheese on toast floating on top or served separately.

🕑 15 minutes

Chilli Tomato Soup

15 g/½ oz/1 tbsp butter or margarine
½ small red onion, chopped
1 red chilli, seeded and finely chopped
½ celery stick, chopped
225 g/8 oz tomatoes, skinned and chopped
10 ml/2 tsp sun-dried tomato purée (paste)
120 ml/4 fl oz/½ cup boiling vegetable or chicken stock
Salt and freshly ground black pepper
15 ml/1 tbsp torn fresh basil leaves
Wholemeal bread or ciabatta rolls, to serve

1 Put the butter or margarine in a bowl and microwave on High for 20 seconds until melted. Add the onion, chilli and celery and microwave on High for 3 minutes, stirring once.

2 Add the tomatoes and microwave on High for 1 minute. Stir in the tomato purée and stock and season to taste with salt and pepper. Microwave on High for 3 minutes.

3 Cover the soup and leave to stand for 1 minute. Stir in the basil and serve the soup piping hot with wholemeal bread or ciabatta rolls.

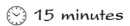 15 minutes

Snacks and Light Meals

Ideas for speedy snacks, brunches and light lunches and late-night munchies can all be found in this chapter. While it's relatively easy to think ahead and shop for your main meal, it's more challenging to consider the light bites in between. Help is at hand with your microwave. No recipe in this section takes longer than 15 minutes to prepare and cook and many take much less.

Warm Brioches with Creamy Mushrooms

15 g/½ oz/1 tbsp butter or margarine
175 g/6 oz baby button mushrooms, halved
60 ml/4 tbsp crème fraîche
10 ml/2 tsp dry sherry
5 ml/1 tsp light soy sauce
15 ml/1 tbsp snipped fresh chives
Salt and freshly ground black pepper
2 French brioches

1 Melt the butter or margarine in a bowl on High for 30 seconds. Add the mushrooms, stir to coat and microwave for a further 2 minutes.

2 Stir in the crème fraîche, sherry, soy sauce, chives and salt and pepper and cook on Medium for 2½ minutes, until the mushrooms are tender and the sauce piping hot.

3 Meanwhile, cut off the tops of the brioches horizontally and scoop out some of the soft middle to make hollows large enough for the mushroom filling.

4 Put the brioches, cut-side up, under a low grill (broiler) to warm through and to crisp the edges, but watch carefully as they burn quickly.

5 Spoon the filling into the warm brioche bases and replace the tops. Serve straight away.

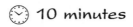 10 minutes

Spicy Pitta Pockets

100 g/4 oz lean minced (ground) lamb
4 spring onions (scallions), finely chopped
1.5 ml/¼ tsp ground coriander (cilantro)
1.5 ml/¼ tsp ground cumin
4 dried apricots, finely chopped
1 white or wholemeal pitta bread
15 ml/1 tbsp chopped fresh coriander
Salt and freshly ground black pepper
30 ml/2 tbsp plain Greek yoghurt

1   Put the lamb and spring onions in a bowl and microwave on High for 2–3 minutes or until cooked, stirring twice during cooking to break up any large pieces of mince.

2   Sprinkle the ground coriander and cumin over and stir in the apricots. Cover and microwave on High for 1 minute. Remove and leave to stand for 2–3 minutes.

3   Cut the pitta widthways. Microwave on High for 30 seconds, then carefully open up to make two pockets.

4   Stir the chopped coriander into the spicy lamb mixture and season to taste with salt and pepper. Divide between the pitta halves and spoon in the yoghurt. Serve straight away.

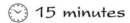 15 minutes

Cheese and Chilli Nachos

12 tortilla chips
25 g/1 oz/¼ cup Cheddar cheese, grated
A pinch of celery salt
1 small red chilli, seeded and finely chopped
60 ml/4 tbsp soured (dairy sour) cream or crème fraîche
15 ml/1 tbsp chopped fresh coriander (cilantro)
Freshly ground black pepper

1 Arrange the tortilla chips around the edge of a serving plate. Sprinkle the cheese, celery salt and chilli over.

2 Microwave, uncovered, on Medium for 2 minutes or until the cheese has melted. Leave to stand for 30 minutes.

3 Meanwhile, mix together the soured cream or crème fraîche, coriander and some pepper. Spoon into a small bowl and place in the middle of the nachos before serving.

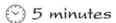 5 minutes

Moules Marinières

225 g/8 oz mussels
15 g/½ oz/1 tbsp butter or margarine
½ small onion, finely chopped
1 small garlic clove, crushed
75 ml/5 tbsp dry white wine or cider
Freshly ground black pepper
15 ml/1 tbsp chopped fresh parsley

1 Wash and scrub the mussels, removing the hairy 'beards' that protrude from the side of the shells Tap any open ones with the back of a knife and discard those that don't close.

2 Put the butter or margarine, onion and garlic in a large bowl and microwave on High for 2 minutes, stirring once

3 Add the wine or cider and microwave on High for 1½ minutes or until boiling.

4 Add the mussels, cover with pierced clingfilm (plastic wrap), then microwave on High for 1½ minutes or until the shells open. Discard any that remain closed.

5 Tip into a serving dish and season with pepper. Sprinkle with the parsley and serve straight away.

⊙ 15 minutes

✴ Mussels are sold by either volume or weight: 225 g/8 oz is the equivalent of 300 ml/½ pt/1¼ cups.

Smoked Chicken and Melted Brie Croissants

2 small croissants
15 g/½ oz/1 tbsp butter or margarine, softened
5 ml/1 tsp Dijon mustard
50 g/2 oz smoked chicken, thinly sliced
50 g/2 oz Brie, thinly sliced
1 tomato, sliced
Salt and freshly ground black pepper

1 With a serrated knife, slice each croissant in half horizontally. Blend together the butter or margarine and mustard and spread thinly over the cut surfaces.

2 Arrange the chicken in two portions on a plate. Top each with the Brie, followed by the tomato slices.

3 Microwave on High for 1 minute or until the cheese is just beginning to melt and the chicken is warm. Season with salt and pepper.

4 Using a spatula, transfer the chicken and cheese to the bottom halves of each croissant. Replace the top halves of the croissants and serve straight away.

🕐 10 minutes

✴ If you like your croissants hot and crusty, place under a low grill (broiler) for about 30 seconds on each side before spreading with mustard butter and filling; watch them carefully as they burn easily.

Avocado Dip

1 streaky bacon rasher (slice), rinded
½ ripe avocado
10 ml/2 tsp lime juice
A pinch of mild chilli powder
Salt and freshly ground black pepper
1 tomato, skinned, seeded and chopped
Tortilla chips, crackers or crusty French bread, to serve

1 Place the bacon on a sheet of kitchen paper (paper towel), cover with another sheet and microwave on High for 1½ minutes until crisp. Leave to cool.

2 Peel and stone (pit) the avocado. Mash the flesh with the lime juice, chilli powder and some salt and pepper.

3 Crumble the bacon into the mixture and add to the avocado with the tomato and a sprinkling of salt and pepper. Mix well, cover and chill for up to 2 hours or until needed.

4 Serve the dip with tortilla chips or crackers or spread on crusty French bread

🕐 5 minutes

✖ To skin the tomato, place in a small bowl and pour over enough boiling water to cover. Drain after 1 minute and rinse under cold water to cool. The skin should then come away easily.

✖ Brush the remaining avocado half with lime juice and leave the stone in place to prevent the flesh turning brown. It will keep in the fridge for up to 2 days.

Smoky Bacon and Cheese Dip

4 smoked streaky bacon rashers (slices), rinded
50 g/2 oz/¼ cup unsalted butter
50 g/2 oz/¼ cup cream cheese
50 g/2 oz/½ cup Gruyère (Swiss) cheese, grated
A pinch of ground paprika
1 spring onion (scallion), chopped
Freshly ground black pepper
Crackers or crudités, to serve

1 Arrange the bacon on a sheet of kitchen paper (paper towel), cover with another sheet and microwave on High for 2 minutes until crisp. Leave to cool, then crumble.

2 Put the butter and cream cheese in a bowl and microwave on Medium for 20 seconds until soft.

3 Mix in the crumbled bacon, Gruyère, paprika and spring onion. Season to taste with pepper. Serve with crackers or crudités.

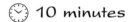 10 minutes

Country Pâté

25 g/1 oz/2 tbsp garlic and herb butter
75 g/3 oz chicken livers
Salt and freshly ground black pepper
A pinch of ground mace
5 ml/1 tsp brandy
Toast, pitta bread or melba toast, to serve

1 Put half the butter in a bowl and microwave on High for 30 seconds to melt.

2 Add the chicken livers, stirring to coat in the butter. Cover and microwave on High for 2 minutes, stirring twice.

3 Season with salt, pepper and the mace. Stir in the brandy, then mash with a fork until as smooth as possible or purée with a hand-held blender.

4 Spoon into an individual dish and smooth the top. Melt the remaining butter in a jug on High for 30 seconds. Pour over the pâté and leave to cool and set.

5 Serve the pâté with fingers of hot toast or pitta bread or melba toast.

🕐 15 minutes

✳ It's worth making a double quantity of this delicious pâté. Cover with clingfilm (plastic wrap) and store in the fridge for up to 3 days.

Smoked Haddock Pâté

Serves 2

150 g/5 oz smoked haddock fillets
25 g/1 oz/2 tbsp butter or margarine
10 ml/2 tsp lemon juice
1 small garlic clove, crushed
A dash of Tabasco sauce
30 ml/2 tbsp Mascarpone cheese
Buttered toast or crusty wholemeal bread, to serve

1 Place the haddock on a plate, dot with the butter or margarine, cover and microwave on High for 5 minutes.

2 Remove the skin and any bones, then purée the fish and any juices in a food processor or mash with a fork until as smooth as possible.

3 Add the remaining ingredients and mix until smooth.

4 Press into individual dishes, cover and chill or freeze in individual portions. Serve with hot buttered toast or crusty wholemeal bread.

⏲ 10 minutes plus chilling

✶ Choose undyed smoked haddock fillets rather than the brightly coloured yellow ones for this pâté, if available.

Mackerel Pot

1 small smoked mackerel fillet
5 ml/1 tsp butter or margarine
5 ml/1 tsp plain (all-purpose) flour
A little mustard powder
75 ml/5 tbsp milk
15 g/½ oz/2 tbsp Cheddar cheese, grated
Freshly ground black pepper
Toast, to serve

1 Remove the skin from the fillet and flake the flesh, discarding any bones.

2 Put the butter or margarine in a bowl and microwave on High for 10 seconds. Stir in the flour and a pinch of mustard powder, then gradually blend in the milk. Microwave on High for 1 minute, whisking halfway through cooking.

3 Stir in the fish and most of the cheese. Season generously with pepper.

4 Spoon into an individual dish. Sprinkle with the reserved cheese and microwave on High for 1 minute until the cheese melts. Serve hot with toast.

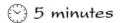 5 minutes

Egg and Cheese Florentine

50 g/2 oz baby spinach leaves
15 g/½ oz/1 tbsp butter or margarine, plus extra for greasing
15 ml/1 tbsp plain (all-purpose) flour
100 ml/3½ fl oz/scant ½ cup milk
25 g/1 oz/¼ cup Cheddar cheese, grated
1 egg
A pinch of grated nutmeg
Salt and freshly ground pepper

1   Put the spinach in a bowl, part-cover and microwave on High for 2 minutes. Squeeze out any excess water and transfer to a well-greased individual dish

2   Put the butter or margarine in a jug and microwave on High for 20 seconds. Stir in the flour, then whisk in the milk. Microwave on High for 1½ minutes, whisking halfway through cooking, until smooth and thick. Stir in the cheese.

3   Make a hollow in the the spinach, break in the egg and season with the nutmeg and salt and pepper. Pour the cheese sauce over and microwave on High for 2 minutes or until the egg is just set and the sauce bubbling.

🕐 10 minutes

Crab Rounds

175 g/6 oz crabmeat
1 spring onion (scallion), sliced
15 ml/1 tbsp mayonnaise
5 ml/1 tsp lemon juice
10 ml/2 tsp chopped fresh parsley
25 g/1 oz/¼ cup Cheddar cheese, grated
Freshly ground black pepper
8 rounds of melba toast
A pinch of ground paprika

1 Mix together the crabmeat, spring onion, mayonnaise, lemon juice and parsley in a small bowl. Stir in the cheese and season with pepper.

2 Line a plate with two layers of kitchen paper (paper towel). Spoon the crab mixture on the toast rounds and arrange on the plate. Sprinkle with the paprika.

3 Microwave on High for about 1 minute until the cheese melts, rearranging once during cooking.

🕑 5 minutes

✴ You can use either fresh or canned crabmeat for this recipe. If you buy canned, tip it into a sieve (strainer), rinse briefly under cold water to remove some of the brine and squeeze dry.

Eggs and Cheese

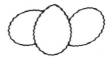

Eggs need care in order to cook them to perfection in the microwave. Conventionally, the white of an egg will cook before the yolk, but because egg yolks contain a high proportion of fat they attract more microwave energy, so cook faster than the white by the microwave method. The 'standing' time given at the end of the recipe is therefore really important here; eggs should look very soft when taken out of the microwave, as they continue cooking for some time in the residual heat. Never put an egg in its shell in the microwave as the steam will build up inside and it will explode.

Cheeses make wonderful sauces, fillings and toppings in the microwave but be careful not to overcook them or they may become stringy.

Smoked Salmon Scramble

15 g/½ oz/1 tbsp butter or margarine
2 eggs
10 ml/2 tsp crème fraîche or single (light) cream
Freshly ground black pepper
5 ml/1 tsp lemon juice
50 g/2 oz smoked salmon, cut into thin strips
10 ml/2 tsp snipped fresh chives
Brown bread or toast, to serve

1 Put the butter or margarine in a bowl and microwave on High for 20 seconds, until half-melted.

2 Whisk together the eggs, crème fraîche or cream and some pepper together. Add to the butter or margarine and microwave on High for 1½ minutes, stirring every 30 seconds, until the mixture is creamy and beginning to set.

3 Sprinkle the lemon juice over the salmon strips and stir into the egg mixture with the chives. Microwave for 15 seconds, then stir again and leave to stand for 30 seconds.

4 Serve straight away with brown bread triangles or hot brown toast, buttered if liked.

⏱ 10 minutes

✷ Buy smoked salmon trimmings for this dish – they are less expensive than slices of smoked salmon. You can use smoked trout instead, if you prefer.

Quick Muffin Pizzas

1 white or wholemeal muffin
1 garlic clove
2 spring onions (scallions), thinly sliced
50 g/2 oz canned tomatoes, drained
5 ml/1 tsp tomato purée (paste)
A large pinch of dried mixed herbs
Freshly ground black pepper
25 g/1 oz peperami sausage stick, sliced, or sliced salami
6 stoned (pitted) black olives
50 g/2 oz Mozzarella cheese, thinly sliced

1 Using a serrated knife, halve the muffin horizontally. Cut the garlic clove in half and gently rub over the cut surfaces of the muffin. Discard the garlic.

2 Put the spring onions, tomatoes, tomato purée and herbs in a bowl and microwave on High for 2 minutes until very thick. Leave to cool.

3 Stir a little pepper into the tomato mixture, then spread over the muffin halves. Arrange the sausage or salami slices on top, then the olives and Mozzarella.

4 Place the pizzas on a serving plate and microwave on High for 1 minute, until the cheese has melted and the muffin halves are hot. Serve straight away.

⏰ 10 minutes

✶ You can use whatever other toppings you have in the fridge; cubes of cooked ham or chicken, crumbled cheeses such as Stilton and Feta, and grated Cheddar or Gruyère (Swiss) cheese all work equally well.

Egg Calypso

10 ml/2 tsp olive oil
½ red onion, very finely chopped
1 small garlic clove, crushed
1 small courgette (zucchini), chopped
200 g/7 oz/1 small can of chopped tomatoes with basil
Salt and freshly ground black pepper
1 egg
10 ml/2 tsp freshly grated Parmesan cheese

1 Put the oil in a small serving dish. Add the onion, garlic and courgette. Stir to coat in the oil, then microwave on High for 2 minutes, stirring once, until softened.

2 Stir in the tomatoes and season with salt and pepper. Microwave on High for 2 minutes, stirring once.

3 Make a small hollow in the middle of the mixture and break in the egg. Carefully prick the yolk with a cocktail stick (toothpick) and sprinkle the cheese over.

4 Microwave on High for 2–2½ minutes, or until the egg is just set. Serve straight away.

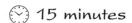 15 minutes

Cheesy Chicken and Spinach Lasagne

Serves 1–2

3 lasagne sheets
10 ml/2 tsp olive oil
½ small onion, very finely chopped
1 small garlic clove, crushed
100 g/4 oz minced (ground) chicken
175 ml/6 fl oz/¾ cup passata (sieved tomatoes)
A large pinch of dried mixed herbs
Salt and freshly ground black pepper
75 g/3 oz frozen leaf spinach, thawed and squeezed dry
50 g/2 oz/¼ cup cottage cheese
For the cheese sauce:
15 g/½ oz/1 tbsp butter or margarine
15 g/½ oz/1 tbsp plain (all-purpose) flour
150 ml/¼ pt/⅔ cup milk
50 g/2 oz/½ cup Cheddar cheese, grated

1 Put the lasagne in a bowl and pour plenty of boiling water over. Cover and microwave on High for 6 minutes. Leave to stand for 10 minutes, then drain and rinse under cold water.

2 Meanwhile, put the oil, onion and garlic in a bowl and stir to coat. Microwave on High for 1 minute.

3 Stir in the chicken and microwave on High for 3 minutes, stirring every minute to separate the lumps of mince.

4 Stir in the passata, herbs and some salt and pepper. Cover with pierced clingfilm (plastic wrap) and microwave on High for 2 minutes. Stir, then re-cover and microwave on Medium for 4 minutes. Stir in the spinach and cottage cheese.

5 Whisk together all the sauce ingredients except the cheese, in a jug. Microwave on High for 3 minutes, whisking every minute, until boiling and thickened. Stir in half the cheese and season to taste.

6 Spoon a third of the chicken mixture into a rectangular dish and top with a sheet of lasagne. Repeat until all the chicken mixture and lasagne is used up.

7 Sprinkle the top with the remaining cheese and microwave on Medium for 2 minutes, then on High for 1 minute or until bubbling. Brown the top under a preheated grill (broiler) if liked. (Make sure the dish you are using is flameproof.) Leave to stand for a few minutes before serving.

⏱ 30 minutes

✷ You can also use minced turkey instead of chicken in this recipe.

✷ It is important to cook the lasagne in step 1 even if you use a no-need-to-precook variety.

Classic Frittata

20 g/¾ oz/1½ tbsp butter or margarine
½ small onion, very finely chopped
1 medium potato, cooked and diced
1 tomato, peeled, seeded and chopped
30 ml/2 tbsp frozen peas, thawed
15 ml/1 tbsp chopped fresh parsley (optional)
2 eggs
15 ml/1 tbsp milk
Salt and freshly ground black pepper
5 ml/1 tsp olive oil

1 Put half the butter or margarine in a bowl with the onion and microwave on High for 2 minutes, stirring halfway through cooking.

2 Add the potato, tomato, peas and parsley if using. Whisk together the eggs and milk. Season with salt and pepper, add to the potato mixture and mix well.

3 Microwave the remaining butter or margarine and the olive oil in an 18 cm/7 in glass pie dish on High for 20 seconds until the butter or margarine melts. Tip the dish so that the base is covered.

4 Spread the egg and potato mixture evenly over the dish. Cover with pierced clingfilm (plastic wrap) and microwave on High for 1 minute.

5 With a fork, push the cooked egg around the edge of the dish to the middle, allowing the uncooked egg to move to the edge.

6 Re-cover and microwave on High for a further 1 minute. Allow to stand for 1 minute, then serve straight away.

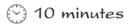 10 minutes

Melted Cheese and Tuna Bagels

2 white or wholemeal bagels
50 g/2 oz/¼ cup cream cheese
15 ml/1 tbsp mayonnaise
½ celery stick, finely chopped
5 ml/1 tsp drained capers
100 g/4 oz canned tuna, drained
Freshly ground black pepper
40 g/1½ oz/⅓ cup Emmenthal or Gruyère (Swiss) cheese,
thinly sliced

1   With a serrated knife, halve the bagels horizontally. Arrange on a serving plate, cut-side up.

2   Put the cream cheese in a bowl and microwave on Low for 30 seconds to soften. Stir in the mayonnaise, celery, capers, tuna and some pepper.

3   Spoon the filling on to the bagel halves. Top with the cheese slices and microwave on High for 1½–2 minutes or until the cheese is just melted and the tuna mixture is warm. Serve straight away.

⏱ 10 minutes

Crustless Ham and Broccoli Quiche

100 g/4 oz broccoli, cut into small florets
50 g/2 oz/½ cup cooked smoked ham, cubed
60 ml/4 tbsp single (light) cream or milk
2 eggs
50 g/2 oz/½ cup Cheddar cheese, grated
Salt and freshly ground black pepper

1   Arrange the broccoli in a 15 cm/6 in flan dish. Cover with pierced clingfilm (plastic wrap) and cook on High for 2½ minutes or until tender, moving the pieces around halfway through cooking. Remove the dish from the microwave and add the ham, placing it between the broccoli florets.

2   Put the cream or milk in a jug and heat on Medium for 45 seconds until bubbling.

3   Meanwhile, whisk the eggs with the cheese and some salt and pepper. Add to the hot cream or milk and mix well. Pour the mixture over the broccoli and ham.

4   Place the flan on a microwave rack and cook on Medium for 8 minutes or until just set. Leave to stand for 2–3 minutes before serving.

🕗 18 minutes

Kohlrabi and Cheese Layer

4 small kohlrabi, peeled
1 bay leaf
15 g/½ oz/1 tbsp butter or margarine, softened
25 g/1 oz/¼ cup mature Cheddar or Leicester cheese, grated
Salt and freshly ground black pepper.
25 g/1 oz/¼ cup toasted chopped walnuts
10 ml/2 tsp chopped fresh parsley

1   Thinly slice the kohlrabi and place in a bowl with the bay leaf. Pour over just enough boiling water to come halfway up the sides of the bowl, cover and microwave on High for 5 minutes or until just tender. Drain thoroughly, discarding the bay leaf.

2   Use the butter or margarine to grease a shallow baking dish. Add the kohlrabi slices in layers, sprinkling a little of the cheese and some salt and pepper between the layers and over the top.

3   Microwave on High for 2 minutes or until the cheese has melted. Leave to stand for 2 minutes, then serve sprinkled with the walnuts and parsley.

🕐 15 minutes

Piperade

100 g/4 oz canned chopped tomatoes, drained
1 small green (bell) pepper, chopped
1 shallot, finely chopped
1 small garlic clove, finely chopped
10 ml/2 tsp olive oil
10 ml/2 tsp chopped fresh oregano
A dash of Tabasco sauce
Salt and freshly ground black pepper
2 eggs, beaten
Buttered toast or crusty farmhouse bread and a green salad,
to serve

1 Mix together the tomatoes, green pepper, shallot, garlic and oil and microwave on High for 3 minutes until soft. Stir in the oregano and Tabasco and season with salt and pepper.

2 Stir the eggs into the vegetable mixture and microwave on Medium for 2½–3 minutes, stirring every 30 seconds, until the mixture is lightly scrambled and creamy.

3 Serve the piperade with buttered toast or crusty farmhouse bread and a green salad.

🕐 10 minutes

✳ Make this quick dish more substantial by stirring in a little chopped cooked ham or a few slivers of salami for the last 30 seconds of cooking.

Fish and Seafood

The microwave, with its high-speed cooking, cooks fish to absolute perfection, retaining its succulence and delicate taste and texture. The moistness of fish means that it can be cooked with little or no added liquid or fat, so that its natural flavour is retained.

Both fish and seafood need the minimum of cooking; a piece of fish can be ready in two to three minutes. When done, the outside should be opaque and the middle still slightly translucent; don't be tempted to microwave it for longer as it will complete cooking on standing.

Mullet in Paper Parcels

1 large or 2 small red mullet fillets, about 100 g/4 oz in all
¼ red (bell) pepper, thinly sliced
¼ red onion, thinly sliced
5 ml/1 tsp olive oil
10 ml/2 tsp lemon juice
Salt and freshly ground black pepper
A sprig of rosemary (optional)

1 Place the mullet skin-side down on a 30 cm/12 in square of baking parchment. (If using two fillets, place them side by side in a single layer.)

2 Put the red pepper and onion in a bowl, sprinkle the oil and lemon juice over and season with salt and pepper. Toss together to mix. Cover with pierced clingfilm (plastic wrap) and microwave on High for 1 minute.

3 Place the pepper and onion on top of the mullet with any juices and the sprig of rosemary, if using. Bring the four corners of the paper together and twist together to make a sealed parcel.

4 Put on a serving plate and cook on High for 1½ minutes or until the fish flakes easily when tested with a fork. Leave to stand for 1 minute before serving.

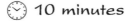 10 minutes

Plaice with Orange and Almonds

15 g/½ oz/2 tbsp toasted flaked (slivered) almonds
25 g/1 oz/½ cup fresh white breadcrumbs
15 ml/1 tbsp chopped fresh parsley
5 ml/1 tsp grated orange rind
Juice of ½ orange
Salt and freshly ground black pepper
2 small plaice fillets, skinned
15 g/½ oz/1 tbsp butter or margarine

1   Roughly crush the almonds and mix together with the breadcrumbs, parsley, orange rind and enough of the orange juice to bind everything together. Season to taste with salt and pepper.

2   Spread the stuffing over the plaice fillets and roll them up from the wider end to the narrow tail end to enclose the stuffing. Secure each with a wooden cocktail stick (toothpick).

3   Place in a small dish and spoon over any remaining orange juice. Dot the tops with the butter or margarine.

4   Cover with pierced clingfilm (plastic wrap) and microwave on High for 2 minutes or until the fish is just opaque and flakes easily. Leave to stand for 2 minutes before serving.

🕐 15 minutes

Scallops with Coriander Pesto

15 g/½ oz/2 tbsp chopped fresh coriander (cilantro)
1 small garlic clove, peeled
15 ml/1 tbsp pine nuts
30 ml/2 tbsp olive oil
Salt and freshly ground black pepper
30 ml/2 tbsp freshly grated Parmesan cheese
4 large shelled scallops
Crusty French bread, to serve

1 To make the pesto sauce, put the coriander, garlic, pine nuts, oil and some salt and pepper in a food processor or blender and process until smooth. Stir in the Parmesan.

2 Cut the corals from the scallops, then slice the white part horizontally through the middle into two rounds.

3 Arrange the white parts in a circle around the edge of a plate. Cover with pierced clingfilm (plastic wrap) and cook on High for 1½ minutes until just turning opaque. Add the reserved corals and cook on High for a further 45–60 seconds until tender.

4 Rearrange the scallops on the plate, draining off any liquid and spoon about half the pesto sauce over. Serve straight away with crusty French bread.

⊙ 10 minutes

✷ Reserve the remaining pesto and store in a screw-topped jar in the fridge for up to a week. It is delicious served with cooked pasta.

Citrus Halibut with Fennel

½ small fennel bulb, thinly sliced
15 ml/1 tbsp lime or lemon juice
1 halibut steak, about 200 g/7 oz
Salt and freshly ground black pepper
15 g/½ oz/1 tbsp butter or margarine
Finely grated rind and juice of ½ orange
30 ml/2 tbsp dry white wine

1 Put the fennel in a bowl and sprinkle with the lime or lemon juice. Cover with clingfilm (plastic wrap) and cook on High for 3–4 minutes or until almost tender.

2 Drain the fennel and arrange in a greased, shallow dish. Place the halibut on top, season with salt and pepper, then dot the top with the butter or margarine.

3 Mix together the orange rind and juice and the wine in a jug or bowl. Microwave on High for 2 minutes to reduce slightly, then pour over the halibut.

4 Cover and microwave on High for 4 minutes or until the fish is opaque and flakes easily with a fork. Leave to stand for 2 minutes before serving.

🕒 15 minutes

Mediterranean-style Swordfish

1 swordfish cutlet, about 150 g/5 oz
1 bay leaf
A strip of pared lemon rind (optional)
30 ml/2 tbsp fish or vegetable stock
30 ml/2 tbsp dry white wine
5 ml/1 tsp olive oil
200 g/7 oz/1 small can of chopped tomatoes
5 ml/1 tsp sun-dried tomato purée (paste)
1 small garlic clove, crushed
10 ml/2 tsp aniseed liqueur such as pastis
5 stoned (pitted) black olives
Salt and freshly ground black pepper
15 ml/1 tbsp torn fresh basil leaves

1 Place the swordfish in a dish. Tuck the bay leaf and lemon rind (if using) underneath. Whisk together the stock, wine and oil and drizzle over. Leave at room temperature while making the sauce.

2 Put all the remaining ingredients except the basil in a bowl. Cover with pierced clingfilm (plastic wrap) and microwave on High for 4 minutes, stirring twice.

3 Cover the swordfish and microwave on High for 3–4 minutes or until the fish is opaque and flakes easily when tested. Remove the fish and pour the juices into the sauce.

4 Reheat the sauce on High for 30 seconds, stir in the basil, pour over the fish and serve straight away.

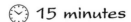 15 minutes

Cod in Cucumber Sauce

100 g/4 oz cod fillet
15 ml/1 tbsp water
Salt and freshly ground black pepper
A slice of lemon
For the sauce:
2 spring onions (scallions), chopped
45 ml/3 tbsp crème fraîche or soured (dairy sour) cream
5 cm/2 in piece of cucumber, finely diced
15 ml/1 tbsp milk
A pinch of grated nutmeg

1　Place the fish in a shallow dish. Sprinkle with the water, season with salt and pepper and top with the lemon slice. Cover and microwave on High for 2–2½ minutes, or until the fish flakes easily when tested with a fork.

2　To make the sauce, place the spring onions in a bowl, cover and microwave on High for 30 seconds.

3　Stir in the remaining ingredients and microwave on Medium for 1½ minutes until hot. Stir well. Pour the sauce over the fish and serve.

🕚 10 minutes

Spicy Oat and Almond Herrings

5 ml/1 tsp tomato purée (paste)
2.5 ml/½ tsp Dijon mustard
A dash of Worcestershire sauce
2 small herring fillets
30 ml/2 tbsp medium oatmeal
15 g/½ oz/2 tbsp almonds, finely chopped
A small pinch of cayenne
Salt and freshly ground black pepper
15 ml/1 tbsp sunflower oil
15 g/½ oz/1 tbsp butter or margarine
Lemon wedges, to serve

1 Combine the tomato purée, mustard and Worcestershire sauce to make a smooth paste. Spread very thinly over the herring fillets.

2 Mix together the oatmeal, almonds, cayenne, salt and pepper and sprinkle over the herrings to coat. Press down lightly.

3 Heat the oil and butter or margarine in a shallow dish for 40 seconds until sizzling. Swirl around the base of the dish, then add the fillets, skin-side down, and cook on High for 1½ minutes.

4 Turn the fillets over and cook the other side on High for 1½ minutes or until the fish flakes easily when tested with a fork. Serve hot with lemon wedges to squeeze over.

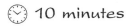 10 minutes

Simple Fish Pie

25 g/1 oz/2 tbsp butter or margarine
10 ml/2 tsp plain (all-purpose) flour
75 ml/5 tbsp milk
100 g/4 oz white fish, skinned
50 g/2 oz cooked peeled prawns (shrimp)
15 ml/1 tbsp chopped fresh dill (dill weed) or parsley
Salt and freshly ground black pepper
50 g/2 oz mashed potato
15 g/1 oz/¼ cup Cheddar cheese, grated
1 tomato, sliced

1 Put half the butter or margarine in a jug and microwave on High for 20 seconds until melted. Stir in the flour, then blend in the milk.

2 Microwave on High for 1–1½ minutes until smooth and thickened, whisking every 30 seconds.

3 Place the fish on a plate, cover with pierced clingfilm (plastic wrap) and microwave on High for 2–3 minutes until just cooked. Flake the fish, removing any bones. Stir into the sauce with the prawns and herbs. Season to taste with salt and pepper.

4 Spoon the fish mixture into an individual serving dish. Melt the remaining butter or margarine on High for 30 seconds and stir into the mashed potato with most of the cheese. Spoon over the fish mixture, then sprinkle with the remaining cheese.

5 Microwave on High for 2–2½ minutes until piping hot. Leave to stand for 1 minute, then arrange the tomato slices over the top and serve.

 15 minutes

Vegetable-topped Fish Fillets

1 skinless fish fillet, about 150 g/5 oz
5 ml/1 tsp lemon juice
1 small courgette (zucchini)
½ small carrot
30 ml/2 tbsp finely grated Parmesan cheese
10 ml/2 tsp sesame seeds
Salt and freshly ground black pepper
Plain rice or buttered new potatoes, to serve

1 Place the fillet, skinned-side down, on a serving plate and sprinkle with the lemon juice.

2 Finely grate the courgette and carrot. Squeeze out the excess liquid, then put into a bowl.

3 Add the cheese and sesame seeds to the bowl, season with salt and pepper and mix well. Arrange on top of the fish fillet, pressing down firmly.

4 Microwave, uncovered, on High for 2½ minutes or until the fish flakes easily when tested with a fork and the vegetables are just tender.

5 Leave to stand for 1 minute before serving with rice or buttered new potatoes.

🕐 **10 minutes**

✳ Salmon, trout, mullet and hoki are all good choices for this dish.

Fish with Rich Tomato Sauce

¼ red (bell) pepper, chopped
½ celery stick, chopped
1 spring onion (scallion), chopped
10 ml/2 tsp olive oil
100 g/4 oz canned chopped tomatoes
5 ml/1 tsp tomato purée (paste)
15 ml/1 tbsp dry white wine or cider
10 ml/2 tsp chopped fresh parsley
A pinch of English mustard powder
Salt and freshly ground black pepper
100 g/4 oz white fish, cubed

1 Put the red pepper, celery, spring onion and oil in a deep dish with a lid and microwave on High for 2–2½ minutes or until tender.

2 Stir in all the remaining ingredients except the fish, cover and microwave on High for 2 minutes. Stir well.

3 Add the fish and microwave, uncovered, on Medium for 3–4 minutes or until the fish is cooked, stirring once during cooking.

🕐 15 minutes

✳ Use thick white fish, such as cod, for this recipe.

Fragrant Fish Curry

10 ml/2 tsp lime juice
A pinch of salt
A pinch of ground turmeric
150 g/5 oz cod fillet, skinned
½ small onion, roughly chopped
1 small garlic clove, crushed
½ green chilli, seeded and roughly chopped
15 g/½ oz/2 tbsp cashew nuts, roughly chopped
75 ml/5 tbsp fish stock or water
15 ml/1 tbsp groundnut or sunflower oil
A pinch of cumin seeds
1.5 ml/¼ tsp ground coriander (cilantro)
75 ml/5 tbsp single (light) cream
15 ml/1 tbsp chopped fresh coriander
Plain rice or naan bread, to serve

1   Mix together the lime juice, salt and turmeric. Rub over the fish fillet, then cut into 5 cm/2 in cubes.

2   Put the onion, garlic, chilli, nuts and the stock or water in a food processor and blend to a paste.

3   Put the oil in a bowl with the cumin seeds and microwave on Medium for 30 seconds. Stir in the onion paste and ground coriander and microwave on High for 3 minutes, stirring once during cooking.

4   Stir in the cream and microwave on High for 1 minute. Stir the fish into the sauce with the fresh coriander. Cover and microwave on High for 3 minutes or until the fish is cooked, stirring twice during cooking. Leave to stand for 1 minute, then serve hot with rice or naan bread.

 15 minutes

Kedgeree

100 g/4 oz smoked haddock fillet
5 ml/1 tsp lemon juice
150 ml/¼ pt/⅔ cup boiling water
15 g/½ oz/1 tbsp butter or margarine
1 spring onion (scallion), chopped
25 g/1 oz/2 tbsp long-grain rice
1 hard-boiled (hard-cooked) egg, chopped
10 ml/2 tsp chopped fresh parsley
Salt and freshly ground black pepper

1   Put the haddock in a shallow dish, sprinkle the lemon juice over, then cover with the boiling water. Microwave on High for 1½–2 minutes or until the fish flakes easily when tested with a fork. Drain, reserving the cooking liquid. Remove the skin from the fish and flake the flesh.

2   Put the butter or margarine in a deep dish with a lid and microwave on High for 20 seconds. Add the spring onion and microwave for 30 seconds.

3   Add the rice, then pour the fish cooking liquid over. Cover and microwave on High for 2 minutes, then on Medium for 9–10 minutes or until the liquid has been absorbed and the rice is tender, stirring once or twice during cooking.

4   Stir in the fish, egg, parsley and salt and pepper to taste. Microwave on High for 30 seconds until heated through. Serve at once.

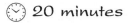 20 minutes

Skate in Creamy Caper Sauce

1 shallot, peeled and roughly chopped
½ celery stick, chopped
1 bay leaf
2 black peppercorns
300 ml/½ pt/1¼ cups water
1 piece of skate wing, about 200 g/7 oz, skinned
15 ml/1 tbsp cider vinegar
45 ml/3 tbsp double (heavy) cream
5 ml/1 tsp capers
10 ml/2 tsp chopped fresh parsley
Salt and freshly ground black pepper

1 Put the shallot, celery, bay leaf and peppercorns in a shallow dish with the water. Cook on High for 4 minutes.

2 Add the skate and 10 ml/2 tsp of the vinegar. Cover and cook on Medium for 3 minutes. Turn the fish over, then cook on Medium for a further 3–4 minutes or until the fish is just cooked. Leave to stand in the water for 1 minute.

3 Meanwhile, put the cream, capers, parsley and some salt and pepper in a small bowl or jug with the remaining vinegar. Cook on High for 30 seconds until bubbling.

4 Lift the skate out of the poaching liquid and transfer to a warmed serving plate. Spoon the cream sauce over and serve straight away.

🕐 15 minutes

✻ The skate is cooked when the flesh comes away easily from the central cartilaginous 'bone'.

Trout with Prawn and Mushroom Stuffing

½ celery stick, chopped
25 g/1 oz button mushrooms, sliced
1 spring onion (scallion), chopped
15 g/½ oz/1 tbsp butter or margarine
2.5 ml/½ tsp finely grated lemon rind
15 ml/1 tbsp chopped fresh parsley
15 ml/1 tbsp chopped fresh dill (dill weed)
30 ml/2 tbsp fresh white breadrumbs
50 g/2 oz small cooked peeled prawns (shrimp)
Salt and freshly ground black pepper
1 medium trout, cleaned

1 Put the celery, mushrooms, spring onion and butter or margarine in a bowl and microwave on High for 2 minutes or until the celery is tender.

2 Stir in the lemon rind, parsley, dill, breadcrumbs and prawns and season well with salt and pepper. Spoon the stuffing into the cavity of the trout.

3 Place the trout on a microwave roasting rack or a plate and cover with greaseproof (waxed) paper. Microwave on Medium for 5–6 minutes or until the fish flakes easily when tested with a fork, turning once halfway through cooking. Serve immediately.

🕒 15 minutes

Monkfish and Prawn Kebabs

175 g/6 oz monkfish tail
4 tiger prawns (jumbo shrimp), peeled
Finely grated rind and juice of ½ small lemon
4 red or yellow cherry tomatoes
½ small red (bell) pepper, cut into chunks
15 g/½ oz/1 tbsp butter or margarine
30 ml/2 tbsp dry white wine
10 ml/2 tsp chopped fresh dill (dill weed) or parsley
Salt and freshly ground black pepper

1   Cut the fish into 4 cm/1½ in chunks and place in a bowl with the prawns. Add half the lemon rind and juice. Stir to coat, then cover and leave to marinate for 15 minutes.

2   Thread the fish, prawns, tomatoes and red pepper on to two soaked, wooden skewers (the soaking prevents the juices from sinking into the skewers during cooking).

3   To make the sauce, put the butter or margarine and white wine in a small jug and microwave on High for 30 seconds. Drizzle 15 ml/1 tbsp over the kebabs.

4   Place the kebabs on a shallow dish, cover with greaseproof (waxed) paper and microwave on High for 3–4 minutes or until the fish is opaque and the prawns are pink. Rearrange halfway through to ensure even cooking.

5   Stir the dill and the remaining lemon rind and juice into the remaining sauce and season to taste. Reheat on High for 15 seconds. Drizzle over the kebabs before serving.

15 minutes plus marinating

Coriander Salmon Cutlet

10 ml/2 tsp balsamic vinegar
10 ml/2 tsp olive oil
2.5 ml/½ tsp clear honey
Salt and freshly ground black pepper
15 ml/1 tbsp chopped fresh coriander (cilantro)
150 g/5 oz salmon cutlet
Lemon wedges, to serve

1 Mix together the vinegar, oil, honey, salt, pepper and coriander in a shallow dish. Add the salmon and turn to coat in the mixture. Cover and marinate for 30 minutes.

2 Cover and microwave on Medium for 2½–3 minutes until the fish flakes easily when tested with a fork. Garnish with lemon wedges and serve straight away.

10 minutes plus marinating

Devilled Crab

15 g/½ oz/1 tbsp butter or margarine
1 spring onion (scallion), chopped
10 ml/2 tsp dry sherry
75 g/3 oz crabmeat
30 ml/2 tbsp fresh wholemeal breadcrumbs
1.5 ml/¼ tsp made English mustard
A few drops of Worcestershire sauce
10 ml/2 tsp chopped fresh parsley
Salt and freshly ground black pepper
15 ml/1 tbsp finely grated Gruyère (Swiss) cheese

1   Put the butter or margarine and spring onion in a shallow dish and microwave on High for 30 seconds.

2   Stir in the sherry, crabmeat, half the breadcrumbs, the mustard, Worcestershire sauce, parsley and some salt and pepper. Microwave on High for 45 seconds.

3   Mix together the remaining breadcrumbs and the cheese and sprinkle over the dish. Microwave on High for about 1 minute until the cheese has melted. Serve at once.

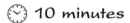 10 minutes

Prawn Pilau

10 ml/2 tsp olive oil
½ red onion, thinly sliced
1 small green chilli, seeded and chopped
1 small garlic clove, crushed
1 bacon rasher (slice), rinded and chopped
25 g/1 oz/2 tbsp long-grain rice
25 g/1 oz French (green) beans, cut into 5 cm/2 in lengths
100 g/4 oz canned chopped tomatoes with basil
120 ml/4 fl oz/½ cup chicken stock
100 g/4 oz cooked peeled prawns (shrimp)
10 ml/2 tsp chopped fresh parsley
Salt and freshly ground black pepper

1 Put the oil and onion in a bowl. Stir to coat, cover and microwave on High for 1 minute. Stir in the chilli, garlic and bacon and microwave on High for 2 minutes until soft.

2 Add the rice, beans, tomatoes and their juice and the stock. Cover and microwave on High for 3 minutes, stirring once.

3 Reduce the power setting to Medium and microwave for 10 minutes, stirring once, until most of the stock has been absorbed and the rice is tender.

4 Stir in the prawns and parsley and season with salt and pepper. Microwave on High for 30 seconds. Leave to stand for 1 minute before serving.

🕐 20 minutes

Gingered Prawns

1 spring onion (scallion), chopped
10 ml/2 tsp grated fresh root ginger
5 ml/1 tsp tomato purée (paste)
5 ml/1 tsp light soy sauce
10 ml/2 tsp dry sherry
A dash of Tabasco sauce
100 g/4 oz cooked peeled prawns (shrimp)

1 Mix together the spring onion, ginger, tomato purée, soy sauce, sherry and Tabasco. Microwave on High for 30 seconds until hot.

2 Stir in the prawns until well coated. Microwave on High for 1 minute until heated through. Serve immediately.

🕐 5 minutes

Poultry

For succulence and flavour, microwaved poultry is hard to beat. Because it is naturally tender, it is ideal for the fast, moist cooking of the microwave oven. It won't, however, brown and crisp skin in the same way as a conventional oven, but you can remedy this by either finishing the dish with a quick flash under a hot grill (broiler) or by taking the healthy option of removing the skin before or after cooking. A delicious way of giving poultry a browned appearance is to brush it with equal quantities of Dijon mustard and Worcestershire sauce blended with a little oil.

When cooking poultry portions, arrange them with the meatier pieces towards the edge of the dish and the thinner piece in the middle. Uneven cooking of boneless chicken breasts can be prevented by tucking the thin ends under. Small whole birds such as poussins (Cornish hens) and quail cook especially well in the microwave and you'll find recipes for them here.

Shredded Sesame Chicken

175 g/6 oz boneless chicken breast, skinned
5 ml/1 tsp sunflower oil
5 ml/1 tsp sesame oil
50 g/2 oz baby button mushrooms, halved
2 spring onions (scallions), trimmed and shredded
5 cm/2 in piece of cucumber, cut into matchsticks
5 ml/1 tsp cornflour (cornstarch)
15 ml/1 tbsp dry sherry
75 ml/5 tbsp chicken stock
5 ml/1 tsp balsamic vinegar
Salt and freshly ground black pepper
10 ml/2 tsp toasted sesame seeds

1   Cut the chicken into thin strips. Put the oils in a bowl, add the chicken and toss to coat. Microwave on High for 1 minute.

2   Stir in the mushrooms, spring onions and cucumber and cook on High for 2 minutes, stirring halfway through cooking.

3   Blend the cornflour with the sherry, stock and vinegar. Stir into the chicken and cook on High for 3–4 minutes, or until the sauce has thickened and the chicken is tender.

4   Season to taste with salt and pepper and serve straight away, sprinkled with the sesame seeds.

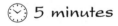 5 minutes

Grapefruit-glazed Chicken

1 chicken portion, skinned
1 small garlic clove, crushed
A pinch of paprika
Salt and freshly ground black pepper
75 ml/5 tbsp unsweetened grapefruit juice
5 ml/1 tsp clear honey
10 ml/2 tsp chopped fresh parsley

1   Place the chicken in a baking dish and make two or three shallow slashes with a sharp knife. Rub the garlic into the slashes and sprinkle with the paprika and a little salt and pepper.

2   Blend together the grapefruit juice and honey and pour over the chicken.

3   Cover and microwave on High for 8 minutes, turning twice during cooking and basting with the grapefruit mixture.

4   Sprinkle with the parsley, cover and leave to stand for 2 minutes before serving.

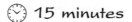 15 minutes

Chicken in Rich Tomato and Mushroom Sauce

50 g/2 oz mushrooms, sliced
1 small onion, sliced
1 garlic clove, crushed
10 ml/2 tsp olive oil
100 g/4 oz canned chopped tomatoes
5 ml/1 tsp tomato purée (paste)
45 ml/3 tbsp dry white wine
1 bay leaf
175 g/6 oz boneless chicken breast, skinned and cubed
Salt and freshly ground black pepper
3 stoned (pitted) black olives, halved lengthways
15 ml/1 tbsp torn fresh basil leaves

1 Put the mushrooms, onion and garlic in a bowl and drizzle the oil over. Stir to coat, then cover and microwave on High for 2½ minutes until soft, stirring once.

2 Stir in the tomatoes, tomato purée, wine, bay leaf and chicken. Season with salt and pepper, cover and microwave on High for 5–6 minutes, stirring once during cooking, until the chicken is cooked and the vegetables are tender.

3 Stir in the olives and basil and leave to stand for 2 minutes. Remove the bay leaf before serving.

🕐 15 minutes

Crunchy Chicken Goujons

60 ml/4 tbsp plain yoghurt
1 garlic clove, crushed
A pinch of fennel seeds, crushed
Salt and freshly ground black pepper
175 g/6 oz boneless chicken breast, skinned
60 ml/4 tbsp dry white breadcrumbs
10 ml/2 tsp freshly grated Parmesan cheese
A pinch of paprika

1 Mix together the yoghurt, garlic, fennel seeds and seasonings. Cut the chicken into strips, stir into the yoghurt mixture and leave to marinate for at least 15 minutes or up to 2 hours, if time allows.

2 Mix the breadcrumbs, Parmesan and paprika on a plate. Lift the chicken strips out of the marinade a few at a time and roll in the crumb mixture, pressing lightly to coat.

3 Arrange the chicken on a roasting rack and microwave on Medium for 3–3½ minutes, turning halfway through cooking, until the chicken is firm and no longer pink.

🕑 10 minutes plus marinating

Golden Chicken with Ginger and Apricots

15 g/½ oz/1 tbsp butter or margarine
5 ml/1 tsp sunflower oil
1 small onion, thinly sliced
2.5 cm/1 in piece of fresh root ginger, peeled
and finely shredded
5 dried apricots, chopped
2 boneless chicken thighs, skinned
150 ml/¼ pt/⅔ cup apple juice
10 ml/2 tsp lemon juice
10 ml/2 tsp light soy sauce
Freshly ground black pepper
30 ml/2 tbsp toasted flaked (slivered) almonds

1   Put the butter or margarine, oil and onion in a bowl and microwave on High for 30 seconds. Stir to coat the onion, then microwave on High for a further 1½ minutes.

2   Stir in the ginger and apricots, then place the chicken thighs on top and pour the apple juice, lemon juice and soy sauce over. Season with pepper, cover and cook on High for 2 minutes.

3   Reduce the power to Medium and microwave for a further 14 minutes, turning the chicken twice and stirring the sauce during cooking, until the chicken is very tender. Allow to stand for 2 minutes before serving sprinkled with the almonds.

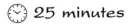 25 minutes

Coq au Vin

15 g/½ oz/1 tbsp butter or margarine
1 shallot, finely sliced
1 small garlic clove, crushed
1 bacon rasher (slice), rinded
5 ml/1 tsp plain (all-purpose) flour
60 ml/4 tbsp chicken stock
60 ml/4 tbsp red wine
5 ml/1 tsp brandy (optional)
1 chicken leg portion, skinned and separated into
thigh and drumstick
50 g/2 oz chestnut mushrooms, sliced
A sprig of thyme
A pinch of dried mixed herbs
Salt and freshly ground black pepper
10 ml/2 tsp chopped fresh parsley

1   Place the butter or margarine in a bowl and microwave on High for 30 seconds to melt. Stir in the shallot and garlic. Cover and microwave on High for 1 minute until soft.

2   Put the bacon on a plate, cover with a sheet of kitchen paper (paper towel) and microwave on High for 1½ minutes until crisp. Crumble the bacon and set aside.

3   Stir the flour into the shallot, then gradually blend in the stock, wine and brandy, if using. Add the chicken pieces and all the remaining ingredients except the parsley.

4   Cover and microwave on High for 8 minutes or until the chicken is tender and cooked through, rearranging the chicken once and stirring the sauce during cooking. Stir in the parsley and leave to stand for 2 minutes before serving.

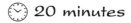 20 minutes

Tarragon Chicken with Mushroom Sauce

15 g/½ oz/1 tbsp butter or margarine
¼ onion, finely chopped
¼ celery stick, finely chopped
1 garlic clove, crushed
45 ml/3 tbsp dried white breadcrumbs
15 ml/1 tbsp chopped fresh tarragon
Salt and freshly ground black pepper
175 g/6 oz boneless chicken breast, skinned
1 egg, beaten
For the sauce:
15 g/½ oz/1 tbsp butter or margarine
75 g/3 oz mushrooms, sliced
30 ml/2 tbsp dry white wine
60 ml/4 tbsp crème fraîche or soured (dairy sour) cream

1 Place the butter or margarine, onion, celery and garlic in a bowl and microwave on High for 2 minutes until soft, stirring halfway through the cooking time. Stir in 15 ml/1 tbsp of the breadcrumbs and the tarragon and season with salt and pepper.

2 Place the chicken breast between two sheets of clingfilm (plastic wrap) or greaseproof (waxed) paper and gently beat to flatten. Spoon the stuffing mixture on top, fold the chicken to surround it and secure with wooden cocktail sticks (toothpicks).

3   Dip the chicken in the egg, then sprinkle with the remaining breadcrumbs to coat. Place in a baking dish and cover with greaseproof paper. Microwave on Medium for 4½–5 minutes until the chicken is cooked through. Leave to stand, still covered, for 3 minutes.

4   Meanwhile, to make the sauce, place the butter or margarine and mushrooms in a bowl and microwave on High for 2 minutes until soft, stirring once. Stir in the wine and crème fraîche or soured cream and season with salt and pepper. Microwave on High for 1½ minutes until bubbling, stirring once during cooking.

⊙ 20 minutes

Chinese Chicken

½ egg white
7.5 ml/1½ tsp cornflour (cornstarch)
A pinch of caster (superfine) sugar
175 g/6 oz boneless chicken breast, skinned and cubed
5 ml/1 tsp groundnut (peanut) or sunflower oil
5 ml/1 tsp toasted sesame oil
25 g/1 oz/¼ cup cashew nuts
A pinch of ground ginger
5 ml/1 tsp dark soy sauce
5 ml/1 tsp dry sherry
1 garlic clove, crushed
Plain rice, to serve

1   Beat the egg white lightly, then mix in the cornflour and sugar. Stir in the chicken pieces and chill for 30 minutes.

2   Lightly grease a plate with the groundnut or sunflower oil. Lift the chicken pieces from the egg white with a slotted spoon and arrange around the edge of the plate. Microwave on High for 4–5 minutes or until just cooked through and tender, turning halfway through cooking.

3   Put the oil and nuts in a separate bowl. Stir, then microwave on High for 45 seconds. Stir in the ginger, soy sauce, sherry, garlic and chicken and microwave on High for 1 minute or until the chicken is hot. Serve with rice.

🕐 15 minutes plus chilling

Chicken Kebabs with Lemon-chive Sauce

15 g/½ oz/1 tbsp butter or margarine
½ small onion, cut into wedges
¼ yellow (bell) pepper, cut into 2.5 cm/1 in pieces
¼ red pepper, cut into 2.5 cm/1 in pieces
175 g/6 oz boneless chicken breast, skinned and cubed
2 bay leaves
For the sauce:
Juice of 1 lemon
25 g/1 oz/2 tbsp butter or margarine, softened
1 egg yolk
Salt and freshly ground black pepper
15 ml/1 tbsp snipped fresh chives

1 To make the kebabs, put the butter or margarine in a shallow dish and microwave on High for 30 seconds until melted. Add the onion and peppers and toss to coat. Cover and microwave on High for 1 minute.

2 Thread the chicken, onion, pepper and bay leaves on two soaked wooden skewers. Place in the dish, cover and microwave on High for 4 minutes or until the chicken is cooked, turning halfway through cooking.

3 Whisk all the sauce ingredients together in a small jug or bowl. Microwave on Medium for 1½ minutes, until thickened, stirring every 30 seconds. Serve with the kebabs.

🕑 15 minutes

Chicken and Broccoli Layer

2–3 slices of wholewheat bread, crusts removed
50 g/2 oz cooked broccoli, cut into small florets
100 g/4 oz/1 cup cooked chicken, chopped
50 g/2 oz/½ cup Gruyère (Swiss) cheese, grated
75 ml/5 tbsp milk
1 small egg, beaten
A pinch of mustard powder
Salt and freshly ground black pepper
15 ml/1 tbsp snipped fresh chives

1 Cut the bread slices into triangles and use to line an individual pie dish. Arrange the broccoli, chicken and half the cheese in layers in the bread-lined dish.

2 Blend together the milk, egg, mustard, seasoning and chives. Pour over the broccoli mixture, cover and leave to soak in the fridge for at least 1 hour.

3 Microwave on High for 2 minutes, then on Medium for 6–8 minutes until a knife inserted in the centre comes out clean. Sprinkle with the remaining cheese and leave to stand for 2 minutes before serving.

🕐 15 minutes plus soaking

Sticky Chicken Drumsticks

2 small chicken drumsticks, skinned
For the marinade:
5 ml/1 tsp Worcestershire sauce
10 ml/2 tsp soft dark brown sugar
5 ml/1 tsp Dijon mustard
10 ml/2 tsp tomato ketchup (catsup)
5 ml/1 tsp sunflower oil

1 Slash the drumsticks several times to allow the marinade to penetrate the flesh.

2 Mix together all the marinade ingredients and thickly brush over the drumsticks. Place in a dish, cover and marinate in the fridge for at least 20 minutes or overnight if preferred.

3 Arrange the drumsticks on a microwave roasting rack or on a plate with the thin ends towards the middle. Microwave on High for 8–10 minutes or until cooked through and tender, turning several times during cooking.

4 Cover with foil and leave to stand for 3–4 minutes to finish cooking, before serving hot, or allow to cool completely and serve cold.

20 minutes plus marinating

✳ Check that the drumsticks are cooked by piercing with a sharp knife or skewer – the juices should run clear. If still pink, microwave for a further minute or so.

Caribbean Chicken

50 g/2 oz canned pineapple chunks in natural juice
5 ml/1 tsp cornflour (cornstarch)
A pinch of mustard powder
A pinch of ground ginger
10 ml/2 tsp soy sauce
10 ml/2 tsp tomato ketchup (catsup)
Salt and freshly ground black pepper
175 g/6 oz boneless chicken breast, cubed
1 small courgette (zucchini), sliced
1 small carrot, chopped
1 spring onion (scallion), finely sliced
Plain rice, to serve

1   Drain the pineapple chunks and reserve 45 ml/3 tbsp of the juice.

2   Blend the juice with the cornflour, mustard, ginger, soy sauce, ketchup and seasoning in a bowl. Stir in the chicken, courgette and carrot.

3   Cover and microwave on High for 5–6 minutes or until the sauce is thick and the meat is tender, stirring twice during cooking.

4   Stir in the spring onion and pineapple chunks, cover and microwave on High for about 1 minute until heated through. Serve hot with rice.

🕒 15 minutes

Orange and Mustard-basted Turkey

100 g/4 oz turkey breast fillet
1 small carrot
For the marinade:
30 ml/2 tbsp orange juice
5 ml/1 tsp soft light brown sugar
5 ml/1 tsp balsamic vinegar
Salt and freshly ground black pepper
For the glaze:
15 ml/1 tbsp orange marmalade
5 ml/1 tsp Dijon mustard

1   Cut the turkey into thin strips and coarsely grate the carrot.

2   Mix together the marinade ingredients, stir in the turkey strips and leave to marinate in the fridge for up to 4 hours.

3   Remove the turkey from the marinade and mix with the carrot.

4   Blend together the glaze ingredients and stir in 5 ml/1 tsp of the marinade.

5   Toss the turkey and carrot in the glaze and microwave on High for 4–5 minutes until the turkey is cooked through, stirring once during cooking.

6   Microwave the remaining marinade on High for 30 seconds or until bubbling. Spoon over the turkey before serving.

 15 minutes plus marinating

Simple Turkey Stroganoff

15 g/½ oz/1 tbsp butter or margarine
½ small onion, very thinly sliced
100 g/4 oz turkey fillet, cut into thin strips
75 g/3 oz mushrooms, sliced
45 ml/3 tbsp chicken stock
75 ml/5 tbsp soured (dairy sour) cream
2.5 ml/½ tsp tomato purée (paste)
2.5 ml/½ tsp wholegrain mustard
2.5 ml/½ tsp paprika
Salt and freshly ground black pepper

1 Put the butter or margarine in a bowl and microwave on High for 30 seconds to melt. Add the onion, stir to coat, then cover and cook on High for 2 minutes or until tender.

2 Stir in the turkey strips, mushrooms and stock. Cover and cook on High for 4 minutes or until the turkey is almost cooked, stirring once during cooking.

3 Add the remaining ingredients and microwave on Medium for 3 minutes, or until the turkey and mushrooms are tender. Leave to stand for 1 minute before serving.

⏲ 15 minutes

✱ Crème fraîche can be used instead of soured cream if preferred. If you are unable to get either, stir 2.5 ml/½ tsp lemon juice into 75 ml/5 tbsp double (heavy) cream and leave to stand at room temperature for 20 minutes before using.

Duck with Black Cherry Sauce

2.5 ml/½ tsp cornflour (cornstarch)
100 g/4 oz canned black cherries in natural juice
30 ml/2 tbsp fruity red wine
10 ml/2 tsp clear honey
2.5 ml/½ tsp Dijon mustard
A pinch of ground ginger
Salt and freshly ground black pepper
1 duck portion

1 Blend the cornflour with a little of the cherry juice, then stir in the wine, honey, mustard, ginger, salt and pepper. Microwave for 30–45 seconds until thickened. Stir in the cherries and set aside.

2 Place the duck on a rack and microwave on Medium for 6–8 minutes until the juices run clear, turning over and draining the fat and basting with a little of the sauce once or twice during cooking. If necessary, shield the bones or narrower portions with small pieces of foil.

3 Spoon the sauce over the duck and leave to stand for 2 minutes before serving.

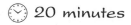 20 minutes

81

Quail in Red Wine

5 ml/2 tsp olive oil
2 oven-ready quail
5 ml/1 tsp chopped fresh thyme
Salt and freshly ground black pepper
2 slices of Parma ham
5 ml/1 tsp balsamic vinegar
75 ml/5 tbsp red wine

1 Rub the oil into the skins of the quail, then sprinkle with the thyme and a little salt and pepper. Wrap each in a slice of Parma ham, securing with wooden cocktail sticks (toothpicks).

2 Place in a shallow dish and pierce the legs and breasts through the ham in several places, with a fine skewer.

3 Pour the vinegar and red wine over, cover with pierced clingfilm (plastic wrap) and microwave on High for 12–15 minutes or until the juices run clear when the thickest part of the birds is pierced with a fine skewer.

4 Place the quail on a warmed serving plate and leave to stand for 5 minutes. Meanwhile, microwave the juices on High for 3 minutes or until syrupy. Pour over the birds before serving.

🕑 25 minutes

✴ To add an extra-special touch, try using olive oil flavoured with lemon or chilli.

Lemon and Pistachio Poussin

25 g/1 oz/2 tbsp butter or margarine, softened
5 ml/1 tsp finely grated lemon rind
15 g/½ oz/2 tbsp skinned pistachio nuts, finely chopped
15 ml/1 tbsp chopped fresh parsley
Salt and freshly ground black pepper
1 oven-ready poussin (Cornish hen), cleaned
A pinch of paprika

1 Reserve 10 ml/2 tsp of the butter or margarine and blend the remainder with the lemon rind, nuts, parsley and some salt and pepper.

2 Gently ease away the poussin skin from the breast and push the flavoured butter or margarine into the pocket, then smooth back the skin.

3 Rub the reserved butter or margarine over the skin, then sprinkle with paprika. Place the poussin in a roasting bag and seal with an elastic band. Pierce a small hole in the bag.

4 Microwave on Medium for 12–15 minutes or until the juices run clear when the thickest part of the thigh is pierced with a fine skewer. Leave to stand, covered, for 5–6 minutes before serving.

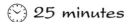 25 minutes

Soy-glazed Duck with Mango Salsa

Juice of 1 small orange
15 ml/1 tbsp dark soy sauce
5 ml/1 tsp soft dark brown sugar
5 ml/1 tsp clear honey
5 ml/1 tsp red wine vinegar
10 ml/2 tsp dry sherry (optional)
5 ml/1 tsp finely chopped fresh root ginger
Freshly ground black pepper
1 boneless duckling breast, about 200 g/7 oz, skinned
1 small or ½ large ripe mango
15 ml/1 tbsp lemon or lime juice
4 spring onions (scallions), finely sliced
1 small fresh red chilli, seeded and finely chopped
15 ml/1 tbsp chopped fresh coriander (cilantro)
1.5 ml/¼ tsp cornflour

1 Blend together the orange juice, soy sauce, sugar, honey, vinegar, sherry, if using, ginger and some pepper.

2 Put the duck in a shallow dish, pour over the marinade, cover and leave to marinate at room temperature for 20 minutes, or overnight in the fridge, if preferred.

3 Meanwhile, to make the salsa, peel, stone (pit) and chop the mango. Put in a small bowl with all the remaining ingredients except the cornflour. Mix well, then cover and set aside until ready to serve.

4 Remove the duckling from the marinade and place on a microwave roasting rack. Microwave on Medium for 6–7 minutes, or until cooked to your liking, turning once during cooking and brushing with the marinade. Leave to stand for 3–4 minutes.

5 Blend the cornflour with the remaining marinade in a jug. Microwave on High for 2 minutes, until thickened and slightly reduced.

6 Cut the duckling diagonally into thick slices. Arrange on a serving plate, drizzle the sauce over and serve with the mango salsa.

🕑 20 minutes plus marinating

Meat

You'll find a wide range of meat dishes in this section, from steaks of beef and gammon to lamb chops, minced (ground) meats, sausages and liver, all ideal for mid-week meals in minutes or delicious dining for special occasions.

Because the microwave cooks in a fraction of the time of conventional cooking, prime tender cuts will produce the best results. You can, however, cook less expensive cuts in curries and casseroles by cooking at a lower microwave power for a longer time.

Special browning dishes are available for the microwave. These should be preheated, so that when the meat is added it sizzles and sears the outside. I have suggested one for Calves' Liver and Onions (see page 94) but, although it gives a brown outer crust to the meat, it is not essential.

Cider-glazed Gammon Steaks

100 g/4 oz middle-cut gammon steak, rinded
75 ml/5 tbsp dry cider
7.5 ml/1½ tsp butter or margarine
50 g/2 oz mushrooms, sliced
2.5 ml/½ tsp cornflour (cornstarch)
15 ml/1 tbsp crème fraîche or soured (dairy sour) cream
15 ml/1 tbsp chopped fresh parsley
Freshly ground black pepper

1   Place the gammon in a shallow dish. Reserve 10 ml/2 tsp of the cider and pour the rest over the gammon. If time allows, cover and leave to marinate for 1 hour.

2   Put the butter or margarine in a bowl and cook on High for 15 seconds. Stir in the mushrooms, cover with pierced clingfilm (plastic wrap) and cook on High for 1½ minutes, stirring halfway through cooking.

3   Cover the dish of gammon with pierced clingfilm and cook on High for 3 minutes or until tender. Strain the juices into the mushrooms. Re-cover the gammon and keep warm.

4   Blend the cornflour with the reserved cider, add to the mushrooms and cook on High for 1 minute until the sauce is bubbling and thickened.

5   Transfer the gammon to a serving plate. Stir the crème fraîche or soured cream and parsley into the sauce and season with pepper. Pour over the gammon and serve straight away.

🕐 15 minutes plus optional marinating

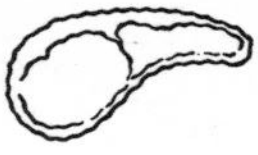

Thai-style Beef

75 ml/5 tbsp coconut milk
2.5 ml/½ tsp soft dark brown sugar
10 ml/2 tsp dark soy sauce
150 g/5 oz rump or sirloin steak, cut into thin strips
1 garlic clove, crushed
½ onion, roughly chopped
1 red chilli, seeded and chopped
10 ml/2 tsp lemon juice
10 ml/2 tsp cornflour (cornstarch)
100 g/4 oz baby spinach leaves, roughly shredded
Salt and freshly ground black pepper

1. Put the coconut milk, sugar and soy sauce in a large bowl and microwave on High for 1 minute. Stir in the steak and cook on High for a further 2 minutes.
2. Meanwhile, process the garlic, onion, chilli, lemon juice and cornflour in a food processor or blender until smooth.
3. Stir the paste into the beef mixture, then cook on Medium for 1 minute.
4. Stir in the spinach and cook on Medium for a further 3–4 minutes or until the meat is tender and the spinach has wilted. Taste and season with salt and pepper before serving.

15 minutes

* When using small quantities of coconut milk in recipes, it's more economical to buy it in powdered form in sachets or use block creamed coconut. Reconstitute according to the packet directions. Canned coconut should be kept in the fridge for a only few days and does not freeze well.

Burgundy Beef

4 small button (pearl) onions
100 g/4 oz medium egg noodles
5 ml/1 tsp sunflower oil
100 g/4 oz lean minced (ground) beef
1 small garlic clove, crushed
1 carrot, sliced
50 g/2 oz mushrooms, sliced
45 ml/3 tbsp beef stock or water
45 ml/3 tbsp dry red wine
5 ml/1 tsp Worcestershire sauce
2.5 ml/½ tsp chopped fresh thyme
1 bay leaf
15 ml/1 tbsp chopped fresh parsley
Salt and freshly ground black pepper

1   Put the onions in a bowl and pour over boiling water to cover. Leave to stand for 5 minutes, then drain and peel.

2   Meanwhile, put the noodles in a bowl, pour over plenty of boiling water and microwave on High for 4 minutes or according to the packet directions. Drain well.

3   Mix together the oil, beef, garlic, carrot and onions. Cover and microwave on High for 2 minutes or until the meat is no longer pink, stirring every 30 seconds.

4   Stir in all the remaining ingredients except the noodles. Cover and microwave on Medium for 10 minutes or until the beef and vegetables are tender, stirring twice.

5   Remove the bay leaf, then stir in the noodles and cook on High for 30 seconds. Leave for 1 minute before serving.

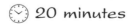 20 minutes

Mexican Beef Tortillas

100 g/4 oz minced (ground) beef
1 shallot, finely chopped
1 red chilli, seeded and finely chopped
1 small garlic clove, crushed
A pinch of ground cumin
A pinch of dried oregano
50 g/2 oz canned chopped tomatoes
Salt and freshly ground black pepper
2 wheat flour tortillas
30 ml/2 tbsp plain Greek yoghurt or crème fraîche
Tomato salad or guacamole, to serve

1 Mix together the beef, shallot, chilli and garlic in a bowl. Cover and microwave on High for 2–2½ minutes or until no longer pink, stirring twice during cooking to break up the mince.

2 Stir in the cumin, oregano, tomatoes and some salt and pepper. Cover and microwave on Medium for 2½ minutes until the flavours blend, stirring once or twice. Leave to stand for 2 minutes.

3 Meanwhile, put the tortillas on a plate and microwave on High for 30 seconds to warm them. Spoon the chilli beef mixture down the centre of each, drizzle the yoghurt or crème fraîche over and serve straight away with a tomato salad or guacamole.

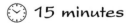 15 minutes

Lamb with Spring Vegetables

10 ml/2 tsp olive oil
1 shallot, finely chopped
1 small garlic clove, crushed
½ celery stick, chopped
100 g/4 oz lamb fillet, cubed
6 baby carrots or turnips, peeled
6 small new potatoes
75 ml/5 tbsp dry white wine
75 ml/5 tbsp vegetable or chicken stock
A small sprig of lemon thyme
1 bay leaf
10 ml/2 tsp chopped fresh mint
Salt and freshly ground black pepper

1 Place the oil, shallot, garlic and celery in a bowl and microwave on High for 1 minute.

2 Add the lamb, stir well, cover and microwave on High for 1 minute.

3 Add the carrots or turnips, potatoes, wine, stock, thyme and bay leaf. Cover and microwave on Medium for 12–15 minutes or until the lamb is tender and the vegetables cooked, stirring once or twice during cooking.

4 Stir in the mint and season with salt and pepper. Leave to stand for 2–3 minutes, then remove the thyme and bay leaf before serving.

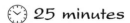 25 minutes

Rich Bolognese Sauce

15 ml/1 tbsp red lentils
75 ml/5 tbsp boiling beef stock
1 small shallot, finely chopped
1 small garlic clove, crushed
1 carrot, chopped
½ celery stick, thinly sliced
10 ml/2 tsp olive oil
100 g/4 oz lean minced (ground) beef
100 g/4 oz canned chopped tomatoes
5 ml/1 tsp sun-dried tomato purée (paste)
30 ml/2 tbsp dry red wine (optional)
A pinch of dried mixed herbs
Salt and freshly ground black pepper
Spaghetti or plain rice, to serve

1   Put the lentils in a small bowl and pour the beef stock over. Cover and leave to soak for at least 5 minutes while preparing the vegetables.

2   Put the shallot, garlic, carrot and celery in a bowl and drizzle with the oil. Stir to mix, then microwave on Medium for 2 minutes.

3   Stir in the beef and microwave on High for 1 minute. Add the soaked lentils, the tomatoes, tomato purée, wine, if using, and herbs. Season with salt and pepper. Cover and microwave on Medium for 12–15 minutes or until the beef and lentils are tender, stirring once during cooking.

4   Leave to stand for 2–3 minutes before serving with spaghetti or rice.

⏱ 20 minutes

✷ The lentils act as a thickener for the sauce, so there's no need to thicken with flour or cornflour (cornstarch) here.

Quick Goulash

15 g/½ oz/1 tbsp butter or margarine
1 small red onion, chopped
1 small garlic clove, crushed
100 g/4 oz rump steak, cut into thin strips
2.5 ml/½ tsp paprika
1.5 ml/¼ tsp caraway seeds
50 g/2 oz canned chopped tomatoes
30 ml/2 tbsp soured (dairy sour) cream or crème fraîche
Salt and freshly ground black pepper

1   Melt the butter or margarine on High for 20 seconds. Add the onion and garlic and stir well. Cover and microwave on Medium for 5 minutes, stirring once or twice.

2   Add the steak and sprinkle the paprika over. Stir, then cover and microwave on Medium for 3 minutes.

3   Stir in the caraway seeds and tomatoes, cover and microwave on Medium for 3–4 minutes or until the meat and onion are tender.

4   Stir in the soured cream or crème fraîche and season to taste. Cover and microwave on Medium for 30 seconds. Leave to stand for 2–3 minutes before serving.

⏱ 20 minutes

Calves' Liver and Onions

10 ml/2 tsp olive oil
2 smoked streaky bacon rashers (slices), rinded and chopped
1 small onion, finely sliced
175 g/6 oz calves' liver, sliced
5 ml/1 tsp cornflour (cornstarch)
100 ml/3½ fl oz/scant ½ cup hot beef stock
5 ml/1 tsp balsamic vinegar
10 ml/2 tsp chopped fresh parsley
Salt and freshly ground black pepper

1 Preheat a browning dish, without the lid, on High for 4 minutes. Add the oil, bacon and onion, stir, then microwave on High for 1 minute.

2 Add the strips of liver to the dish. Cover with the lid and microwave on Medium for 3 minutes, stirring after 1½ minutes.

3 Blend the cornflour to a paste with a little cold water, then stir in the stock and vinegar. Pour over the liver, cover and cook on High for 1½ minutes, stirring every 30 seconds, until the liver is just cooked.

4 Stir in the parsley and season with salt and pepper. Cover and leave to stand for 2–3 minutes before serving.

🕐 15 minutes

✳ Lambs' liver may be used for this recipe if preferred. Soak in a little milk, drain and pat dry on kitchen paper (paper towels) to improve the flavour before slicing.

Italian Meatballs

For the meatballs:
75 g/3 oz lean minced (ground) pork
75 g/3 oz minced ham
30 ml/2 tbsp fresh white breadcrumbs
1 shallot, finely chopped
5 ml/1 tsp tomato purée (paste)
5 ml/1 tsp chopped fresh oregano
1 egg yolk
Salt and freshly ground black pepper
For the sauce:
5 ml/1 tsp olive oil
1 small garlic clove, crushed
½ stick celery, finely chopped
200 g/7 oz/1 small can of chopped tomatoes with basil
Buttered tagliatelle, to serve

1 Mix together all the ingredients for the meatballs in a bowl. Shape into 5 cm/2 in balls and place on a plate lined with greaseproof (waxed) paper.

2 Cover with greaseproof paper and microwave on High for 5–6 minutes until cooked through, rearranging at least once during cooking. Remove and set aside.

3 To make the sauce, put the oil, garlic and celery in a shallow dish and microwave on High for 1 minute. Add the tomatoes and microwave on Medium for 4 minutes. Season with salt and pepper.

4 Arrange the meatballs on top of the sauce in the dish. Cover and microwave on Medium for 1 minute. Serve on a bed of buttered tagliatelle.

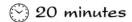 20 minutes

Lamb Pasanda

15 ml/1 tbsp sunflower oil
25 g/1 oz/¼ cup unsalted cashew nuts or almonds
1 small onion, finely sliced
1 garlic clove, crushed
5 ml/1 tsp grated fresh root ginger
2.5 ml/½ tsp ground coriander (cilantro)
A pinch of chilli powder
A pinch of ground cumin
A pinch of ground cardamom
A pinch of ground turmeric
A pinch of ground cloves
100 g/4 oz lean lamb, cubed
60 ml/4 tbsp lamb or vegetable stock
60 ml/4 tbsp coconut milk
60 ml/4 tbsp double (heavy) cream
15 ml/1 tbsp chopped fresh coriander
Salt and freshly ground black pepper

1   Put 5 ml/1 tsp of the oil in a bowl with the nuts and microwave on High for 30 seconds. Tip into a food processor or blender with the half the onion, the garlic, ginger and a little water and blend to a purée.

2   Put the remaining oil and onion in a bowl. Stir, then microwave on High for 1 minute. Add the nut paste, spices and meat and microwave on High for 2 minutes.

3   Stir in the stock, coconut milk and cream, cover and microwave on Low for 12–15 minutes.

4   Stir in the chopped coriander and season with salt and pepper. Leave to stand for 2–3 minutes before serving.

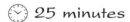 25 minutes

Lamb in Tomato Sauce with Courgettes

100 g/4 oz minced (ground) lamb
1 shallot, chopped
1 garlic clove, crushed
1 small courgette (zucchini), thinly sliced
175 ml/6 fl oz/¾ cup passata (sieved tomatoes)
5 ml/1 tsp chopped fresh marjoram
Salt and freshly ground black pepper
Plain rice or pasta, to serve

1 Mix together the lamb, shallot and garlic and microwave on High for 2½ minutes, stirring every 30 seconds to break up the mince.

2 Stir in the remaining ingredients. Cover and microwave on High for 2 minutes, then on Medium for 5–6 minutes until the courgettes are tender, stirring several times during cooking.

3 Leave to stand for 2 minutes before serving with rice or pasta.

🕐 15 minutes

Herby Lamb with Aubergine

1 small aubergine (eggplant)
1.5 ml/¼ tsp salt
10 ml/2 tsp olive oil, plus extra for greasing
175 g/6 oz lean minced (ground) lamb
1 shallot, finely chopped
1 garlic clove, crushed
50 g/2 oz button mushrooms
2.5 ml/½ tsp chopped fresh rosemary
2.5 ml/½ tsp chopped fresh thyme
75 ml/5 tbsp lamb or vegetable stock
2.5 ml/½ tsp cornflour (cornstarch)
10 ml/2 tsp red wine or cold water
5 ml/1 tsp tomato purée (paste)
Salt and freshly ground black pepper
75 ml/5 tbsp plain Greek yoghurt
1 egg

1 Halve the aubergine lengthways and slash the pulp deeply without breaking the skin. Sprinkle with the salt and leave to stand for 30 minutes.

2 Rinse the aubergine halves under cold, running water and pat dry with kitchen paper (paper towels). Brush the cut surfaces with the oil. Microwave on High for 2½ minutes.

3 Scoop the pulp into a bowl and reserve the skins. Chop the pulp coarsely, then microwave on High for 1 minute. Tip into a colander and drain. Put the aubergine skins in an oiled, shallow dish.

4 Place the lamb, shallot, garlic, mushrooms, rosemary and thyme in a separate bowl and microwave on High for 2 minutes, stirring every 30 seconds to break up the mince.

5   Pour in the stock. Blend the cornflour with the wine or water and stir into the meat mixture with the tomato purée. Add the aubergine pulp. Microwave on High for 1 minute until thickened. Season with salt and pepper.

6   Spoon the mixture into the aubergine shells. Mix together the yoghurt and egg and spoon on top of the meat mixture. Microwave on Medium for 5 minutes until the topping is lightly set.

🕒 20 minutes plus standing

Simple Stir-fried Pork

5 ml/1 tsp groundnut (peanut) oil
100 g/4 oz pork fillet, cut into thin strips
1 garlic clove, crushed
2 spring onions (scallions), chopped
5 ml/1 tsp cornflour (cornstarch)
15 ml/1 tbsp dark soy sauce
10 ml/2 tsp sweet sherry
15 ml/1 tbsp orange juice
5 ml/1 tsp grated fresh root ginger
50 g/2 oz mangetout (snow peas), halved lengthways
50 g/2 oz beansprouts
Plain rice or noodles, to serve

1 Mix together the oil, pork, garlic and spring onions in a bowl. Microwave on High for 2 minutes, stirring once during cooking.

2 Blend the cornflour with the soy sauce, sherry, orange juice and ginger. Add to the bowl with the mangetout. Microwave on High for 1½ minutes.

3 Stir in the beansprouts and microwave on High for 1 minute or until the pork is cooked and the vegetables are just tender. Serve with rice or noodles.

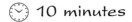 10 minutes

Gingered Lamb Chop

15 g/½ oz/1 tbsp butter or margarine
2.5 ml/½ tsp lemon juice
2.5 ml/½ tsp finely grated lemon rind
2.5 ml/½ tsp grated fresh root ginger
Salt and freshly ground black pepper
1 lamb chump chop
1 sprig of rosemary (optional)

1   Place the butter or margarine in a small bowl and microwave on High for 10 seconds until softened. Add the lemon juice and rind, ginger and some salt and pepper.

2   Place the chop in a shallow dish, with the thinner end towards the middle, and brush the butter or margarine over both sides. Bruise the rosemary, if using, and tuck it under the chop.

3   Microwave on High for 2½–3 minutes until the chop is cooked, to your liking, turning once during cooking.

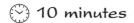 10 minutes

Sausage and Apple Bake

2 pork sausages
1 small onion, thinly sliced
1 eating (dessert) apple, peeled and thinly sliced
1 shallot, finely chopped
15 g/½ oz/1 tbsp butter or margarine
5 ml/1 tsp plain (all-purpose) flour
2.5 ml/½ tsp Dijon mustard
A dash of Worcestershire sauce
A dash of Tabasco sauce
5 ml/1 tsp soft dark brown sugar
10 ml/2 tsp balsamic vinegar
75 ml/5 tbsp tomato juice
Salt and freshly ground black pepper

1　Prick the sausages and arrange in a dish. Cover and microwave on High for 1½ minutes. Remove from the dish.

2　Stir the onion into the juices in the dish, cover and microwave on High for 2 minutes. Add the apple and toss together gently. Microwave on High for 45 seconds.

3　To make the sauce, place the shallot and butter or margarine in a small bowl and microwave on High for 1½ minutes, stirring after 30 seconds. Stir in the flour, then blend in all the remaining ingredients.

4　Microwave on High for 3 minutes, stirring twice.

5　Pour the sauce over the sausages and microwave on High for 1 minute, then serve.

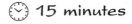 15 minutes

Veal with Marsala Sauce

25 g/1 oz chestnut mushrooms, sliced
60 ml/4 tbsp vegetable or chicken stock
30 ml/2 tbsp marsala wine
100 g/4 oz veal steak, about 1 cm/½ in thick
15 ml/1 tbsp crème fraîche
10 ml/2 tsp chopped fresh parsley
Salt and freshly ground black pepper

1 Mix together the mushrooms, stock and wine in a dish. Cover and microwave on High for 1½ minutes or until the mushrooms are tender, stirring once during cooking.

2 Add the veal, submerging it in the mixture. Cover and microwave on Medium for 3 minutes or until the veal is tender. Remove the veal and keep covered.

3 Stir the crème fraîche, parsley and salt and pepper to taste into the mushroom mixture. Microwave, uncovered, on High for 1 minute or until the sauce bubbles. Pour over the veal to serve.

 10 minutes

Side Dishes, Salads and Vegetarian

The microwave excels at cooking vegetables and, once tried, you may never return to cooking them conventionally again. Quick cooking in only a little additional water means that they will be both tender and crisp, retaining their colour as well as nutrients. Because their water content is high, they literally cook in their own juices. You will also be able to cook small quantities with the minimum of effort and without steaming up the kitchen.

Because vegetables vary in size and density, you should cut them into even-sized pieces when possible and stir or rearrange larger chunks during cooking.

Warm New Potato Salad with Poppyseed Dressing

2 smoked streaky bacon rashers (slices), rinded
100 g/4 oz new potatoes, cut into 2.5 cm/1 in dice
15 ml/1 tbsp water
5 ml/1 tsp poppyseeds
2.5 ml/½ tsp Dijon mustard
15 ml/1 tbsp olive oil
5 ml/1 tsp white wine vinegar
Salt and freshly ground black pepper

1 Place the bacon on a plate and cover with a sheet of kitchen paper (paper towel). Microwave on High for 1½–2 minutes or until crisp. Allow to cool, then crumble.

2 Put the potato cubes and water in a bowl. Cover with pierced clingfilm (plastic wrap) and microwave on High for 3½ minutes, stirring once. Leave to stand for 2 minutes, then drain well

3 Meanwhile, whisk together the poppyseeds, mustard, oil, vinegar, salt and pepper Drizzle over the potatoes and toss to coat. Sprinkle with the crumbled bacon before serving.

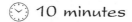 10 minutes

Shredded Carrots with Orange and Coriander

150 g/5 oz carrots, finely shredded
A pinch of coriander (cilantro) seeds, crushed
15 ml/1 tbsp freshly squeezed orange juice
7.5 ml/1½ tsp butter or margarine
15 ml/1 tbsp chopped fresh coriander
Salt and freshly ground black pepper

1 Put the carrots, crushed coriander seeds, orange juice and butter or margarine in a shallow serving dish.

2 Cover with a lid or plate and microwave on High for 3 minutes, or until tender, stirring once during cooking.

3 Stir in the chopped coriander and season well with salt and pepper before serving.

🕐 **10 minutes**

✴ For speed, use the largest grating attachment on a food processor to shred the carrots, or buy ready-shredded from the supermarket.

Fresh Fennel in Tomato Sauce

½ fennel bulb
15 ml/1 tbsp vegetable stock or water
200 g/7 oz/1 small can of peeled tomatoes, drained and chopped
1 shallot, very thinly sliced
1.5 ml/¼ tsp garlic purée (paste)
10 ml/2 tsp chopped fennel fronds or fresh dill (dill weed)
Salt and freshly ground black pepper

1   Cut the fennel from the stalk to the root end into thin wedges. Put in a bowl with the stock or water, cover with pierced clingfilm (plastic wrap) and microwave on High for 2½ minutes. Drain thoroughly.

2   Add the remaining ingredients, season to taste with salt and pepper, then stir to coat the fennel.

3   Cover and microwave on High for 4–5 minutes, stirring once, until the fennel is tender and the sauce bubbling.

4   Allow to stand, still covered, for 2–3 minutes before serving.

🕐 15 minutes

✴   Keep the drained juice from the tomatoes and store in the fridge for up to a week, or freeze if preferred. It can be added to a soup, sauce or casserole.

Potato Wedges with Mascarpone

175 g/6 oz large new potatoes, scrubbed
30 ml/2 tbsp vegetable stock or water
5 ml/1 tsp lemon juice
10 ml/2 tsp olive oil
30 ml/2 tbsp snipped fresh chives
30 ml/2 tbsp Mascarpone cheese
Sea salt flakes and freshly ground black pepper

1 Slice each potato in half lengthways, then each half lengthways again. Put the wedges in a bowl with the stock or water, lemon juice and oil and toss briefly to coat.

2 Cover the bowl with a plate or pierced clingfilm (plastic wrap) and microwave on High for 5–6 minutes, stirring halfway through cooking, until the potatoes are just tender when tested with a fine skewer.

3 Leave to stand, still covered, for 1 minute, then drain off any juices. Add the chives and Mascarpone and salt and pepper to taste. Stir to coat in the cheese.

4 Re-cover and microwave on High for 20 seconds. Serve hot, or barely warm if preferred.

⏱ **15 minutes**

✳ Choose an oval-shaped variety of new potato if possible for this dish, such as Charlotte or Belle de Fontenay.

Mixed Vegetable Curry

10 ml/2 tsp sunflower oil
1 small garlic clove, crushed
½ small onion, finely sliced
2.5 ml/½ tsp ground coriander (cilantro)
2.5 ml/½ tsp ground cumin
A small pinch of ground turmeric
100 g/4 oz cauliflower florets
50 g/2 oz French (green) beans, trimmed and halved
1 carrot, cut into matchsticks
60 ml/4 tbsp vegetable stock
2.5 ml/½ tsp garam masala
15 ml/1 tbsp chopped fresh coriander
30 ml/2 tbsp plain Greek yoghurt
Plain rice or naan bread, to serve

1 Put the oil, garlic and onion in a bowl. Cover with pierced clingfilm (plastic wrap) and microwave on High for 1 minute.

2 Stir in the ground coriander, cumin and turmeric. Add the cauliflower, beans, carrot and stock. Re-cover and microwave on High for 3 minutes.

3 Stir in the garam masala, re-cover and cook for a further 2–3 minutes or until the vegetables are tender.

4 Add the fresh coriander and yoghurt, stir to mix, then serve straight away with rice or naan bread.

🕐 12–15 minutes

Cheat's Bean Cassoulet

15 g/½ oz/1 tbsp butter or margarine
75 g/3 oz button mushrooms, quartered
100 g/4 oz canned haricot beans, drained
200 g/7 oz/1 small can of chopped tomatoes
1.5 ml/¼ tsp paprika
1.5 ml/¼ tsp dried mixed herbs
1 bay leaf
Salt and freshly ground black pepper
40 g/1½ oz/¾ cup fresh wholemeal breadcrumbs
30 ml/2 tbsp freshly grated Parmesan cheese

1 Put the butter or margarine and mushrooms in a dish and microwave on High for 1 minute, stirring halfway through cooking to coat the mushrooms.

2 Add the beans, tomatoes, paprika, herbs and bay leaf and season with salt and pepper. Stir to mix, then cover with pierced clingfilm (plastic wrap) and microwave on Medium for 5 minutes or until the mushrooms are tender and the mixture is bubbling. Discard the bay leaf.

3 Mix together the breadcrumbs and cheese and sprinkle over the cassoulet. Microwave on High for 30 seconds, or brown under a hot grill (broiler) – make sure the dish is flameproof – for 1–2 minutes until the topping is crisp and browned, if preferred.

🕐 *10 minutes*

Lemon Artichokes

1 globe artichoke
½ lemon, thinly sliced
15 g/½ oz/1 tbsp butter or margarine

1 Trim the artichoke so that it will stand upright. Snip the tips of the leaves and remove the lower leaves. Rinse well.

2 Quarter the lemon slices and tuck into the outer leaves of the artichoke with the rind at the top. Wrap in clingfilm (plastic wrap) and microwave on High for 3 minutes, or until the leaves can be easily pulled off the base and the base is tender.

3 Put the butter or margarine in a small bowl and microwave on High for 20 seconds until melted. Serve with the artichoke for dipping.

🕐 10 minutes

French Beans with Chilli and Coriander

100 g/4 oz French (green) beans, topped and tailed
1 red chilli, seeded and finely chopped
15 g/½ oz/1 tbsp butter or margarine
5 ml/1 tsp lime or lemon juice
10 ml/2 tsp chopped fresh coriander (cilantro)
Salt and freshly ground black pepper

1 Mix the beans with the chilli, butter or margarine and lime or lemon juice. Cover and microwave on High for 3 minutes.

2 Stir in the coriander and season with salt and pepper. Cover and microwave on High for 1 minute or until the beans are just tender but still crisp.

3 Leave to stand for 1 minute and toss well before serving.

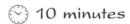 10 minutes

Garlic Mushrooms and Broccoli

100 g/4 oz baby button mushrooms
100 g/4 oz broccoli, cut into small florets
45 ml/3 tbsp vegetable stock
10 ml/2 tsp sunflower oil
5 ml/1 tsp toasted sesame oil
1 small garlic clove, crushed
10 ml/2 tsp balsamic vinegar
Salt and freshly ground black pepper
5 ml/1 tsp sesame seeds

1 Place the mushrooms, broccoli and stock in a bowl. Cover and microwave on High for 1 minute until just beginning to soften but still crisp. Drain well

2 Whisk together the oils, garlic and vinegar and season with salt and pepper Pour over the vegetables and toss together well. Sprinkle with the sesame seeds before serving.

🕐 5 minutes

✦ This dish is equally good served cold. After adding the dressing, allow to cool, then cover and chill in the fridge for up to 8 hours Stir, then sprinkle with the sesame seeds before serving.

Minted Carrots

2 carrots, cut into strips
15 ml/1 tbsp dry white wine
15 g/½ oz/1 tbsp butter or margarine
5 ml/1 tsp chopped fresh mint
Salt and freshly ground black pepper

1 Place the carrots and wine in a bowl, cover and microwave on High for 2 minutes or until just tender. Drain.

2 Add the butter or margarine and microwave on High for 30 seconds. Mix in the mint and season with salt and pepper. Toss together before serving.

🕐 5 minutes

✳ Orange juice can be substituted for the wine, if preferred.

Spicy Salami Mushrooms

15 g/½ oz/1 tbsp butter or margarine
1 shallot, finely chopped
1 garlic clove, crushed
50 g/2 oz mushrooms, sliced
50 g/2 oz spicy salami, diced
10 ml/2 tsp snipped fresh chives
10 ml/2 tsp dry white wine or vegetable stock
30 ml/2 tbsp crème fraîche
Salt and freshly ground black pepper

1 Place the butter or margarine, shallot and garlic in a bowl and microwave on High for 1 minute.

2 Add the mushrooms and salami and microwave on High for 1 minute.

3 Stir in the remaining ingredients, cover and microwave on High for 2 minutes until the sauce is bubbling and the mushrooms are tender.

🕑 5 minutes

Lyonnaise Potatoes

100 g/4 oz potatoes, thinly sliced
A pinch of freshly grated nutmeg
Salt and freshly ground black pepper
15 g/½ oz/1 tbsp butter or margarine
5 ml/1 tsp plain (all-purpose) flour
120 ml/4 fl oz/½ cup milk or single (light) cream
or a mixture of the two
5 ml/1 tsp snipped fresh chives

1 Arrange the potato slices in a shallow dish, slightly overlapping them and sprinkling a little nutmeg, salt and pepper between the layers.

2 Put the butter or margarine, flour and milk and/or cream in a jug. Stir, then microwave on High for 1½ minutes, whisking every 30 seconds. Pour over the potatoes.

3 Cover and microwave on Medium for 10 minutes or until the potatoes are tender. Leave to stand for 2 minutes, then sprinkle with the chives before serving.

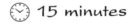 15 minutes

Jacket Potato

1 baking potato, about 225 g/8 oz, scrubbed
2.5 ml/½ tsp sunflower oil
A pinch of salt
Butter or margarine, grated cheese or crème fraîche and snipped
fresh chives, for topping

1 Prick the potato skin all over with a fork and wrap the potato in kitchen paper (paper towels).

2 Microwave on High for 4 minutes, then remove the kitchen paper, rub the skin with the oil and sprinkle with salt. Microwave for a further minute or two or until the potato feels soft when gently squeezed.

3 Wrap the potato in foil, shiny-side in, and leave to stand for 5 minutes.

4 Cut a cross in the top of the potato. Top with butter or margarine, grated cheese, crème fraîche and snipped chives or the filling of your choice (see following recipes).

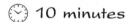 10 minutes

Blue Cheese and Tuna Potato

15 g/½ oz/1 tbsp butter or margarine
2 spring onions (scallions), sliced
½ celery stick, finely chopped
1 large baked potato (see page 117)
45 ml/3 tbsp soured (dairy sour) cream
Salt and freshly ground black pepper
100 g/4 oz canned tuna in oil, drained
75 g/3 oz/¾ cup blue cheese such as Stilton, crumbled

1   Put the butter or margarine, spring onions and celery in a bowl and microwave on High for 1½ minutes until tender, stirring once.

2   Halve the potato lengthways and hollow out to make two potato shells. Add the scooped-out potato to the vegetables.

3   Mash in the soured cream and some salt and pepper. Stir in the tuna and half the cheese. Pile the mixture back into the potato shells and sprinkle with the remaining cheese.

4   Microwave on High for 1–2 minutes until heated through and the cheese has melted.

 10 minutes

Mushroom-stuffed Potato

15 g/½ oz/1 tbsp butter or margarine
1 small garlic clove, crushed
75 g/3 oz baby button or chestnut mushrooms
15 ml/1 tbsp snipped fresh chives
50 g/2 oz/¼ cup Mascarpone cheese
Salt and freshly ground black pepper
1 large baked potato (see page 117)

1 Put the butter or margarine in a bowl and microwave on High for 30 seconds.

2 Stir in the garlic and mushrooms, cover and microwave on High for 2 minutes or until the mushrooms are tender, stirring halfway through cooking.

3 Stir the chives and Mascarpone into the mushrooms and season generously with salt and pepper.

4 Cut a cross in the top of the baked potato and, holding it with a clean cloth, gently squeeze the sides to open up. Spoon the filling on top and serve straight away as the Mascarpone starts to melt.

🕐 10 minutes

✳ Chestnut mushrooms have a slightly stronger flavour than ordinary ones, but either variety can be used for this recipe.

Chilli-spiced Potato Wedges

1 baking potato, about 200 g/7 oz, scrubbed
20 g/¾ oz/1½ tbsp butter or margarine
1 red or green chilli, seeded and finely chopped
A pinch of dried mixed herbs
A pinch of ground cumin
Sea salt and freshly ground black pepper

1 Cut the potato lengthways into eight wedges. Put the butter or margarine in a bowl and microwave on High for 30 seconds until melted. Stir in the chilli, herbs, cumin and salt and pepper to taste.

2 Add the potato wedges and turn to coat in the mixture. Arrange around the edge of a serving plate.

3 Microwave on High for 4 minutes or until the potatoes are tender, rearranging once or twice during cooking.

4 Cover and leave to stand for 2 minutes before serving.

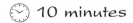 10 minutes

Mixed Vegetables in Herby Tomato Sauce

15 g/½ oz/1 tbsp butter or margarine
1 shallot, finely chopped
1 courgette (zucchini), thinly sliced
½ yellow (bell) pepper, chopped
50 g/2 oz mushrooms, quartered
200 g/7 oz/1 small can of chopped tomatoes
15 ml/1 tbsp mixed fresh herbs, such as chives, basil
and parsley
Salt and freshly ground black pepper

1   Put the butter or margarine and shallot into a bowl. Cover and microwave on High for 30 seconds.

2   Stir in the courgette, yellow pepper and mushrooms. Cover and microwave on High for 3–4 minutes until the vegetables are almost tender, stirring once during cooking.

3   Stir in the remaining ingredients, cover and microwave on Medium for 2 minutes or until the sauce is hot and bubbling, stirring once during cooking.

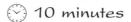 10 minutes

Avocado and Brie Melt

15 ml/1 tbsp olive oil
5 ml/1 tsp tarragon vinegar or lemon juice
2.5 ml/½ tsp wholegrain mustard
A pinch of caster (superfine) sugar
Salt and freshly ground black pepper
1 small avocado
50 g/2 oz Brie
Salad leaves, to garnish

1   Whisk together the oil, vinegar or lemon juice, mustard, sugar and some salt and pepper.

2   Halve, stone (pit), peel and thinly slice the avocado. Cut the Brie into thin slivers. Arrange alternately on a small serving plate.

3   Microwave on Medium for 2 minutes until the avocado is warm and the cheese is starting to melt. Drizzle the dressing over and serve straight away, garnished with salad leaves.

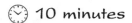 10 minutes

Pasta, Rice and Grains

The range of pastas, rices and grains now available seems endless and it would be impossible to feature them all here. The pasta and rice aisles in supermarkets are full of bright shapes and colours and no longer limited to spaghetti, macaroni and white rice. Grains such as polenta, couscous and bulghar (cracked wheat) are no longer seen as unusual foods and feature in everyday cooking. They also have a long shelf life, so keep a good variety of them in your storecupboard and you'll never be short of ingredients or ideas for delicious meals.

Simple Microwave Pasta

50 g/2 oz fresh pasta or dried pasta
About 600 ml/1 pt/2½ cups boiling water
2.5 ml/½ tsp olive oil
A pinch of salt

1   Place the pasta in a large bowl and pour the boiling water over – the bowl should be no more than half-full. Add the oil and salt and stir.

2   Cover loosely and microwave on High. For fresh pasta, allow 2 minutes for egg noodles or tagliatelle, 3 minutes for spaghetti and 6 minutes for ravioli. For dried pasta, allow 4 minutes for egg noodles, 6 minutes for tagliatelle, 9 minutes for spaghetti or pasta shapes.

3   After cooking, the pasta should be almost tender. If it's still hard, cook for a further 30 seconds, then test again.

4   Allow to stand, covered for 3–4 minutes to finish cooking before draining and serving.

🕐 10–15 minutes

✶   Although microwaving pasta is no quicker than cooking the conventional way, it should be left to stand before serving, giving you time to cook the rest of the meal.

Simple Microwave Rice

50 g/2 oz/¼ cup long-grain rice
150 ml/¼ pt/⅔ cup boiling water
A pinch of salt
A knob of butter or margarine (optional)

1   Rinse the rice in a sieve (strainer) under cold, running water, then tip into a large bowl. Pour the boiling water over. Add the salt and the butter or margarine, if using.

2   Cover loosely and microwave on High for 3 minutes. Stir, then re-cover and microwave on Medium for 7–8 minutes until just tender.

3   Allow to stand, covered, for 2–3 minutes, before fluffing up with a fork.

⏱ 15 minutes

✳ Cook brown rice in the same way, but microwave on High for 3 minutes, then on Medium for 20 minutes.

Spiced Couscous

4 spring onions (scallions), finely sliced
5 ml/1 tsp harissa (hot chilli paste)
5 ml/1 tsp olive oil
1.5 ml/¼ tsp ground cumin
1.5 ml/¼ tsp ground turmeric
200 ml/7 fl oz/scant 1 cup boiling vegetable stock
50 g/2 oz/⅓ cup quick-cook couscous
15 g/1 oz dried raisins or chopped dried apricots
25 g/1 oz/¼ cup pine nuts, toasted
5 ml/1 tsp lemon juice
15 ml/1 tbsp chopped fresh coriander (cilantro) or parsley
White or wholemeal pitta bread, to serve

1 Put the spring onions, harissa, oil, cumin and turmeric in a bowl. Stir, then microwave on High for 30 seconds.

2 Pour in the boiling stock, then add the couscous in a steady stream, stirring all the time. Cover with pierced clingfilm (plastic wrap) and microwave on High for 2 minutes.

3 Stir in the dried fruit, pine nuts and lemon juice. Re-cover and microwave on High for a further 30 seconds.

4 Leave to stand for 1 minute, then stir in the coriander or parsley and serve hot with white or wholemeal pitta bread.

⏱ **10 minutes**

✳ This dish is equally good served cold, with chopped, fresh fruit stirred in.

Classic Italian Risotto

15 g/½ oz/1 tbsp butter or margarine
2 spring onions (scallions), halved and shredded
50 g/2 oz/¼ cup risotto rice
A pinch of saffron powder or strands
200 ml/7 fl oz/scant 1 cup boiling vegetable stock
45 ml/3 tbsp dry white wine
15 g/½ oz Parmesan cheese, thinly shaved
Salt and freshly ground black pepper

1   Put the butter or margarine in a bowl and microwave on High for 20 seconds until melted. Stir in the spring onions, rice and saffron and microwave on High for 30 seconds.

2   Stir in a quarter of the hot stock. Microwave on High for 2 minutes or until all the liquid is absorbed. Repeat this process three more times until all the liquid is absorbed and the rice is almost tender.

3   Heat the wine in a small jug or bowl for 20 seconds, then stir into the rice. Microwave on High for 1 minute or until absorbed and the rice is tender. Stir in half of the Parmesan and season well with salt and pepper. Cover and leave to stand for 1 minute.

4   Spoon the risotto on to a serving plate and serve hot, scattered with the remaining Parmesan shavings.

🕒 15 minutes

Polenta Pizza

50 g/2 oz/½ cup plain (all-purpose) flour
2 5 ml/½ tsp baking powder
1.5 ml/¼ tsp salt
50 g/2 oz/⅓ cup polenta
1.5 ml/¼ tsp dried mixed herbs
1 egg
15 ml/1 tbsp milk
15 ml/1 tbsp olive oil
For the topping:
15 ml/1 tbsp sun-dried tomato purée (paste)
5 ml/1 tsp chopped fresh oregano
4 tomatoes, skinned and chopped
50 g/2 oz/½ cup Mozzarella cheese, thinly sliced
6 stoned (pitted) black olives

1 Sift the flour, baking powder and salt into a mixing bowl. Stir in the polenta and herbs.

2 Beat together the egg, milk and oil and add to the dry ingredients. Mix together to make a soft dough. Turn out on to a lightly floured surface and knead for a few seconds until smooth.

3 Cut out a round of baking parchment about 23 cm/9 in in diameter. Pat out the dough on the paper to a round about 20 cm/8 in in diameter. Place directly on the microwave turntable.

4 Microwave, uncovered, on High for 3 minutes until the dough is firm on top and around the edges.

5 Blend together the tomato purée and oregano and spread over the pizza base. Top with the chopped tomatoes, followed by the sliced Mozzarella and the olives.

6 Microwave, uncovered, on Medium for 3 minutes, or until the cheese is melted and bubbling. Leave to stand for 2 minutes before serving.

🕔 **20 minutes**

✱ Add your favourite topping to the pizza, if liked.

Kofta Lamb

30 ml/2 tbsp bulghar (cracked wheat)
30 ml/2 tbsp boiling water
1 shallot, very finely chopped
1 small garlic clove, crushed
100 g/4 oz lean minced (ground) lamb
15 ml/1 tbsp chopped fresh mint
1.5 ml/¼ tsp ground cumin
Salt and freshly ground black pepper
Pitta bread and salad, to serve

1 Put the bulghar in a bowl and spoon the boiling water over. Cover with pierced clingfilm (plastic wrap) and leave to soak for 1 minute, then microwave on Medium for 20 seconds. Leave to stand for 5 minutes.

2 Add all the remaining ingredients and mix well until combined. Divide the mixture into three equal portions and shape each into a sausage about 10 cm/4 in long

3 Arrange round the edge of a plate and microwave, uncovered, on High for 2½ minutes, turning once during cooking. Allow to stand for 1 minute before serving in a warmed and split pitta bread with salad.

🕔 **10 minutes**

Fresh Pasta with Smoked Trout

½ smoked trout, about 100 g/4 oz
5 ml/1 tsp lemon juice
100 g/4 oz fresh pasta such as tagliatelle
Salt and freshly ground black pepper
100 g/4 oz thin asparagus tips
60 ml/4 tbsp crème fraîche
20 ml/1½ tbsp chopped fresh dill (dill weed)
A sprig of dill, to garnish (optional)

1   Remove and discard the skin and bones from the trout and break into large flakes. Sprinkle with the lemon juice and set aside.

2   Put the pasta in a bowl, season with a little salt, then pour over enough boiling water to come 2.5 cm/1 in above the pasta. Cover with pierced clingfilm (plastic wrap) and microwave on High for 2 minutes. Leave to stand, covered, while finishing the dish.

3   Put the asparagus tips in a single layer in a rectangular dish. Sprinkle 45 ml/3 tbsp water over, cover with pierced clingfilm and microwave on High for 2 minutes until just tender, then drain.

4   Drain the pasta and return to the bowl with the asparagus, trout, crème fraîche, chopped dill and salt and pepper to taste. Gently toss together to mix, then re-cover and microwave on High for 30 seconds until piping hot. Serve garnished with a sprig of dill, if liked.

 15 minutes

Wholewheat Spaghetti with Fresh Tomato Sauce

100 g/4 oz fresh wholewheat spaghetti
600 ml/1 pt/2½ cups boiling vegetable stock
10 ml/2 tsp olive oil
½ small onion, very finely chopped
1 small garlic clove, crushed
100 g/4 oz ripe plum tomatoes, skinned, seeded and chopped
5 ml/1 tsp chopped fresh oregano
Salt and freshly ground black pepper
30 ml/2 tbsp freshly grated Parmesan cheese

1   Put the spaghetti in a large bowl and pour the stock over. Cover with pierced clingfilm (plastic wrap) and microwave on High for 3 minutes. Leave to stand, still covered, while making the sauce.

2   Put the oil, onion and garlic in a bowl, stir, then microwave on High for 2–2½ minutes until softened. Stir in the tomatoes and 45 ml/3 tbsp of the stock from the spaghetti. Cover with pierced clingfilm and microwave on High for 1 minute.

3   Stir in the oregano and season to taste with salt and pepper. Microwave, uncovered, on High for 30 seconds.

4   Drain the spaghetti and place on a serving plate and spoon the tomato sauce over. Serve straight away, sprinkled with the Parmesan.

🕐 15 minutes

Jambalaya

1 small onion, peeled and chopped
1 small garlic clove, crushed
½ green (bell) pepper, diced
½ celery stick, chopped
15 ml/1 tbsp olive oil
75 g/3 oz/⅓ cup long-grain rice
1.5 ml/¼ tsp mild chilli powder
A pinch of ground ginger
A pinch of cayenne pepper
150 ml/¼ pt/⅔ cup boiling vegetable stock
5 ml/1 tsp tomato purée (paste)
50 g/2 oz cooked chorizo sausage, cut into small cubes
75 g/3 oz peeled prawns (shrimp), thawed if frozen
15 ml/1 tbsp chopped fresh parsley
Salt and freshly ground black pepper

1 Put the onion, garlic, green pepper and celery in a bowl. Drizzle the oil over, then stir to coat. Microwave on High for 3 minutes, stirring once.

2 Stir in the rice and spices and microwave on High for 20 seconds.

3 Add the stock and tomato purée, cover with pierced clingfilm (plastic wrap) and microwave on High for 2 minutes. Stir, then re-cover and microwave on Medium for 10 minutes or until almost all the stock has been absorbed and the rice is tender.

4 Stir in the chorizo, prawns and parsley and season to taste with salt and pepper. Microwave on High for 30 seconds. Allow to stand for 3–4 minutes before serving.

⏱ 20 minutes

Pasta Primavera

50 g/2 oz penne
2.5 ml/½ tsp olive oil
Salt and freshly ground black pepper
20 g/¾ oz/1½ tbsp butter or margarine
100 g/4 oz asparagus tips
1 small carrot, thinly sliced diagonally
1 small courgette (zucchini), thinly sliced diagonally
50 g/2 oz baby button mushrooms, halved
5 ml/1 tsp finely grated lemon rind
30 ml/2 tbsp Mascarpone cheese
10 ml/2 tsp chopped fresh mint

1 Put the penne in a bowl and pour over enough boiling water to come 5 cm/2 in above the pasta. Add the oil and a pinch of salt. Cover with pierced clingfilm (plastic wrap) and microwave on High for 8 minutes. Leave to stand for 4 minutes, then drain thoroughly.

2 While the pasta is standing, put the butter or margarine and 15 ml/1 tbsp water in a bowl and microwave on High for 20 seconds. Add the vegetables, cover with pierced clingfilm and microwave on High for 3–4 minutes, or until just tender. Drain.

3 Add the pasta, lemon rind and Mascarpone. Stir until the cheese has melted, then microwave on High for 30 seconds. Stir in the mint and season to taste with salt and pepper. Serve straight away.

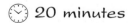 20 minutes

Two-cheese Tagliatelle

100 g/4 oz fresh tagliatelle
Salt
7.5 ml/1½ tsp butter or margarine
1 small garlic clove, crushed
25 g/1 oz/¼ cup Stilton cheese, crumbled
45 ml/3 tbsp crème fraîche
Freshly ground black pepper
25 g/1 oz/¼ cup mature Cheddar cheese, grated
25 g/1 oz/¼ cup chopped walnuts

1 Put the tagliatelle in a bowl, add a pinch of salt, then pour enough boiling water over to come about 2.5 cm/1 in above the pasta. Cover with pierced clingfilm (plastic wrap) and microwave on High for 2 minutes until just tender. Leave to stand, covered, for 2 minutes, then drain thoroughly.

2 Meanwhile, put the butter or margarine and garlic in a bowl and microwave on High for 20 seconds.

3 Add the Stilton and stir in the crème fraîche. Microwave on High for a further 20 seconds. Add the pasta and season with pepper.

4 Sprinkle half the Cheddar over the pasta and gently toss to coat in the sauce. Turn on to a serving plate and serve sprinkled with the remaining Cheddar and the walnuts.

🕐 10 minutes

Tomato and Bacon Macaroni

50 g/2 oz macaroni
2 bacon rashers (slices), rinded and chopped
10 ml/2 tsp tomato purée (paste)
120 ml/4 fl oz/½ cup passata (sieved tomatoes)
15 ml/1 tbsp chopped fresh parsley
A pinch of sugar
Salt and freshly ground black pepper
15 ml/1 tbsp freshly grated Parmesan cheese

1   Put the macaroni in a large bowl and pour enough boiling water over to come 2.5 cm/1 in above the pasta. Cover loosely and microwave on High for 9 minutes. Leave to stand for 3–4 minutes before draining.

2   Place the bacon in a serving dish and microwave on High for 2–3 minutes until crisp. Drain and set the bacon aside.

3   Stir the tomato purée, passata, parsley, sugar and some salt and pepper into the serving dish, cover and microwave on High for 3 minutes.

4   Stir in the cooked macaroni and the bacon, then sprinkle with the cheese. Cover and microwave on High for 1 minute until hot.

🕐 15 minutes

Easy Vegetable Rice

15 g/½ oz/1 tbsp butter or margarine
1 celery stick, thinly sliced
½ small red (bell) pepper, chopped
50 g/2 oz/¼ cup long-grain rice
A pinch of saffron powder or strands
300 ml/½ pt/1¼ cups boiling vegetable or chicken stock
25 g/1 oz frozen broad (fava) beans or peas, thawed
Salt and freshly ground black pepper

1   Put the butter or margarine, celery and red pepper in a bowl. Cover with pierced clingfilm (plastic wrap) and microwave on High for 2 minutes, stirring once.

2   Add the rice, saffron and boiling stock. Stir once, then re-cover and microwave on High for 2 minutes. Reduce the power to Medium and microwave for 10 minutes, stirring once.

3   Stir in the beans or peas and season with salt and pepper Leave to stand, covered, for 3 minutes before serving.

⏱ 20 minutes

Hot Bulghar Salad with Lemon Dressing

40 g/1½ oz/⅓ cup bulghar (cracked wheat), rinsed
150 ml/¼ pt/⅔ cup hot vegetable stock
20 ml/1½ tbsp olive oil
10 ml/2 tsp lime or lemon juice
¼ cucumber, very finely chopped
2 plum tomatoes, peeled, seeded and chopped
1 spring onion (scallion), finely sliced
10 ml/2 tsp chopped fresh mint
10 ml/2 tsp chopped fresh parsley
Salt and freshly ground black pepper
Warm wholemeal or white pitta bread, to serve

1 Put the bulghar in a bowl and pour the stock over. Cover and microwave on Medium for 3 minutes. Remove and leave to stand for 15 minutes, then drain well. Return to the microwave and cook on High for 1 minute

2 Meanwhile, whisk together the oil and lemon juice in a small jug Drizzle over the hot bulghar, then add all the remaining ingredients and mix thoroughly.

3 Serve the salad straight away with warm wholemeal or white pitta bread.

🕐 20 minutes

✳ This is equally delicious served at room temperature. Drizzle the dressing over the warm bulghar and allow to cool before adding the remaining ingredients.

Desserts and Bakes

There's no need to forego desserts or to resort to buying only shop-made biscuits (cookies) and cakes just because you are cooking for one.

Your microwave can provide you with a wealth of new delicious desserts and traditional puddings cooked in minutes rather than hours. Fruit desserts are especially good as the fruit retains its colour, shape and natural fresh flavour. Smooth, creamy custards and the richest of rice puddings cook with great success. Sponge puddings literally rise before your eyes and an all-in-one mixture can be made from scratch to steaming hot on the table in around 10 minutes, rather than simmering on the hob for over an hour.

You'll also find a mouthwatering selection of bakes here – light-textured and moist cakes and both elegant and everyday biscuits.

Nutty Chocolate Banana

1 ripe banana
100 g/4 oz/1 cup plain (semi-sweet) chocolate
15 ml/1 tbsp golden (light corn) syrup
30 ml/2 tbsp chopped mixed nuts

1 Slice the banana in half lengthways and place in a bowl.

2 Break the chocolate into pieces and place in a bowl with the syrup. Microwave on Medium for 1–1½ minutes until the chocolate has melted. Stir until smooth.

3 Spoon the chocolate over the banana and sprinkle with the nuts. Leave to cool, then chill until the chocolate is firm. Serve with ice cream.

🕒 5 minutes plus chilling

Blushing Pears

1 ripe pear
75 ml/5 tbsp fruity red wine
75 ml/5 tbsp water
15 ml/1 tbsp caster (superfine) sugar
A small piece of cinnamon stick
1 whole clove
A pinch of freshly grated nutmeg
A thin strip of pared lemon rind
5 ml/1 tsp lemon juice
15 ml/1 tbsp flaked (slivered) almonds, preferably toasted
Vanilla ice cream or crème fraîche, to serve

1 Cut the pear in half, thinly peel and remove the core with a teaspoon.

2 Put the wine, water, sugar, spices, lemon rind and juice in a dish and microwave on High for 2 minutes.

3 Lay the pear halves in the dish with the thin ends to the centre. Microwave on High for 1–2 minutes until softened. Leave to stand for 2 minutes.

4 Remove the spices and lemon rind. Sprinkle the pear halves with the almonds and serve warm with vanilla ice cream or crème fraîche.

⊘ 10 minutes

✳ These pears are also good served cold. Allow to cool in the syrup, then cover and chill in the fridge for up to 24 hours or until ready to serve.

Strawberry and Rhubarb Crumble

100 g/4 oz rhubarb, cut into chunks
10 ml/2 tsp plain (all-purpose) flour
100 g/4 oz strawberries, sliced
For the topping:
15 ml/1 tbsp rolled oats
15 ml/1 tbsp plain (all-purpose) flour
30 ml/2 tbsp soft light brown sugar
15 ml/1 tbsp granulated sugar
A pinch of ground cinnamon
A pinch of grated nutmeg
15 g/½ oz/1 tbsp butter or margarine
Cream or ice cream, to serve

1 Put the rhubarb into a deep dish and sprinkle with the flour.
   Stir to coat. Cover and microwave on High for 3–4 minutes
   until tender, stirring once. Stir in the strawberries.

2 Mix together the topping ingredients, rubbing in the butter or
   margarine until the mixture resembles breadcrumbs.

3 Sprinkle the topping over the fruit and microwave on Medium
   for 4–5 minutes until bubbling in the centre. Serve with cream
   or ice cream.

🕓 12–15 minutes

Chocolate Sponge Pudding with Hot Fudge Sauce

Serves 1–2

50 g/2 oz/¼ cup soft tub margarine, plus extra for greasing
50 g/2 oz/¼ cup caster (superfine) sugar
1 egg
50 g/2 oz/½ cup self-raising (self-rising) flour
15 ml/1 tbsp cocoa (unsweetened chocolate) powder
1.5 ml/¼ tsp baking powder
15 ml/1 tbsp milk
For the sauce:
15 g/½ oz/1 tbsp butter or margarine
50 g/2 oz/¼ cup soft light brown sugar
45 ml/3 tbsp evaporated milk

1 Put the soft margarine, caster sugar and egg in a mixing bowl. Sift the flour, cocoa and baking powder over. Add the milk, then beat together until smooth and creamy.

2 Spoon the mixture into a well-greased 450 ml/¾ pt/2 cup glass or china pudding bowl and level the top.

3 Microwave on High for 3 minutes or until well risen and just firm to the touch. Leave to stand for 2–3 minutes while making the sauce.

4 Put the butter or margarine and sugar in a jug and microwave on High for 1 minute. Stir in the evaporated milk and microwave on High for 30 seconds.

5 Carefully loosen the sides of the pudding with a palette knife. Turn out on to a serving plate and pour the hot fudge sauce over.

🕓 10 minutes

✱ Serve the pudding with custard or cream instead of the hot fudge sauce, if preferred.

Orange-glazed Pineapple

30 ml/2 tbsp orange marmalade
15 ml/1 tbsp pineapple or orange juice
3 fresh or canned pineapple slices
10 ml/2 tsp dark rum (optional)

1 Mix together the marmalade and pineapple or orange juice. Microwave on High for 30 seconds until melted. Stir until smooth.

2 Brush the pineapple slices with the marmalade mixture and microwave on High for about 1 minute until hot. Spoon the rum over before serving, if using.

🕓 5 minutes

Mocha Mousse

50 g/2 oz/½ cup plain (semi-sweet) chocolate
10 ml/2 tsp brewed espresso or strong black coffee
5 ml/1 tsp brandy
5 ml/1 tsp unsalted (sweet) butter, softened
1 egg, separated

1 Break the chocolate into small squares and place in a bowl with the coffee and brandy. Microwave on Medium for 1 minute until melted.

2 Stir, then blend in the butter, followed by the egg yolk.

3 Whisk the egg white until stiff, then fold into the mixture. Pour into a serving dish and leave to set in the fridge.

5 minutes plus chilling

✳ A different spirit such as rum or an orange or coffee liqueur may be used instead of the brandy if preferred. Alternatively, you can omit the alcohol altogether and add an extra 5 ml/ 1 tsp coffee.

Fresh Figs in Vanilla-scented Syrup

100 ml/3½ fl oz/scant ½ cup water
30 ml/2 tbsp caster (superfine) sugar
½ vanilla pod
2 slightly under-ripe fresh figs
Plain Greek yoghurt, to serve

1 Put the water in a small bowl with the sugar. Split the vanilla pod lengthways and scrape the seeds into the bowl. Add the vanilla pod. Microwave on High for 3 minutes.

2 Meanwhile, wash the figs and pierce the skins several times with a sharp skewer. Cut in half and add to the syrup. Cook on Medium for 2 minutes or until very tender.

3 Allow to stand for 2 minutes before serving warm with Greek yoghurt. Alternatively, remove the figs from the syrup and set aside to cool. When the syrup is cold, pour over the figs and serve with the yoghurt

🕒 10 minutes plus cooling (optional)

Mascarpone and Brazil Nut Nectarine

1 firm ripe nectarine
15 ml/1 tbsp maple syrup
A pinch of ground cinnamon
30 ml/2 tbsp Mascarpone cheese
5 ml/1 tsp Amaretto or orange-flavoured liqueur
2 amaretti biscuits (cookies), crushed
15 ml/1 tbsp flaked (slivered) brazil nuts

1 Halve the nectarine, remove the stone (pit) and place the two halves cut-sides up on a serving plate. Brush with 5 ml/1 tsp of the maple syrup and sprinkle with the cinnamon.

2 Microwave on High for 1 minute until the fruit is very tender and hot.

3 Blend the Mascarpone with the liqueur and the remaining maple syrup. Spoon on top of the hot fruit halves, then sprinkle the biscuits and brazil nuts over. Serve straight away as the Mascarpone begins to melt.

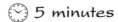 5 minutes

Really Creamy Rice Pudding

25 g/1 oz/2 tbsp round-grain (pudding) rice
15 ml/1 tbsp caster (superfine) sugar
175 ml/6 fl oz/¾ cup milk
120 ml/4 fl oz/½ cup evaporated milk
25 g/1 oz/3 tbsp sultanas (golden raisins)
A pinch of grated nutmeg

1 Put the rice, sugar and milks in a bowl. Cover with pierced clingfilm (plastic wrap) and microwave on High for 3 minutes, stirring once.

2 Stir, then cover and microwave on Medium for 25 minutes, stirring twice during cooking.

3 Stir in the sultanas and nutmeg and leave to stand, covered, for 3–4 minutes before serving.

☼ 35 minutes

✻ Adding evaporated milk to the pudding gives it a very creamy flavour, but all milk may be used instead. Other dried fruit such as apricots or dates are equally delicious in this dish.

Tropical Fruit Pudding with Creamy Custard

Serves 2

25 g/1 oz chopped dried mango or pineapple
20 ml/4 tsp pineapple or orange juice
50 g/2 oz/¼ cup butter or margarine,
plus extra for greasing
50 g/2 oz/¼ cup golden caster (superfine) sugar
1 egg
50 g/2 oz/½ cup self-raising (self-rising) flour
1.5 ml/¼ tsp baking powder
15 ml/1 tbsp desiccated (shredded) coconut
For the custard:
7.5 ml/1½ tsp custard powder
15 ml/1 tbsp caster sugar
150 ml/¼ pt/⅔ cup milk

1 Put the mango or pineapple in a bowl and spoon the pineapple or orange juice over. Microwave on Medium for 30 seconds.

2 Put the butter or margarine, sugar and egg in a mixing bowl. Sift the flour and baking powder over and add the coconut and juices from the warmed fruit. Beat together until smooth and creamy. Fold in the fruit.

3 Spoon the mixture into a well-greased 450 ml/¾ pt/2 cup glass or china pudding bowl and level the top.

4 Microwave on High for 3 minutes or until well risen and just firm to the touch. Leave to stand for 2–3 minutes while making the custard.

5 Mix the custard powder with the sugar and a little of the milk in a jug until smooth. Blend in the remaining milk. Microwave on High for 2½ minutes until smooth and thick, whisking every minute.

6 Turn out the pudding on to a serving plate. Serve straight away with the custard.

🕐 15 minutes

Panettone Bread and Butter Pudding

40 g/1½ oz/3 tbsp butter or margarine, softened
100 g/4 oz panettone, cut into 5 mm/¼ in thick slices
A pinch of grated nutmeg
15 g/½ oz caster (superfine) sugar
150 ml/¼ pt/⅔ cup milk
1 egg, beaten

1 Use 15 ml/1 tbsp of the butter or margarine to grease a shallow serving dish and spread the remainder on the panettone.

2 Cut the panettone into triangles and arrange in the dish, then sprinkle with the nutmeg.

3 Put the sugar and milk in a jug and microwave on High for 30 seconds until warm. Whisk in the egg, then slowly pour over the panettone slices. Leave to soak for 2 minutes.

4 Microwave on Medium for 5–6 minutes, or until the custard is just set. Leave to stand for 2–3 minutes before serving hot or warm.

🕐 15 minutes

Spiced Carrot Cake with Mascarpone Frosting

Makes 8 slices

100 g/4 oz carrots, coarsely grated
30 ml/2 tbsp orange juice
50 g/2 oz/¼ cup butter or margarine
100 g/4 oz/½ cup soft light brown sugar
2 eggs, lightly beaten
150 g/5 oz/1¼ cups self-raising (self-rising) flour
2.5 ml/½ tsp ground cinnamon
1.5 ml/¼ tsp ground ginger
A pinch of grated nutmeg
25 g/1 oz/¼ cup ground almonds
75 g/3 oz/¾ cup walnuts, finely chopped
For the frosting:
250 g/9 oz/1 tub of Mascarpone cheese
5 ml/1 tsp finely grated orange rind
30 ml/2 tbsp icing (confectioners') sugar, sifted

1 Line a 20 cm/8 in round deep dish with clingfilm (plastic wrap). Put the carrots and orange juice in a small bowl, cover and microwave on High for 4 minutes. Leave to cool.

2 Cream together the butter or margarine and sugar until light and fluffy. Gradually add the eggs, beating well after each addition. Sift the flour and spices over and fold into the mixture with the carrots, almonds and walnuts.

3 Spoon the mixture into the prepared dish, level the top and cook on High for 6–7 minutes until well risen and firm to the touch – it should still be slightly moist. Leave to stand for 5 minutes before turning out and cooling on a wire rack. Remove the clingfilm when cold.

4 To make the frosting, mix together all the ingredients and spread over the top and sides of the cake.

5 Cut into wedges to serve.

🕒 15 minutes

Honey Crunch

1 crisp eating (dessert) apple, peeled, cored and sliced
30 ml/2 tbsp clear honey
15 g/½ oz/1 tbsp butter or margarine
25 g/1 oz/2 tbsp muesli

1 Arrange the apple slices in a dish and drizzle half the honey over.

2 Place the butter or margarine in a bowl and microwave on High for 20 seconds until melted. Stir in the remaining honey and the muesli.

3 Sprinkle the mixture over the apples and microwave on High for 4 minutes.

🕒 10 minutes

Winter Fruit Compôte

100 g/4 oz/⅔ cup dried fruit, such as apple rings, peaches, pears,
apricots and prunes
150 ml/¼ pt/⅔ cup apple juice or water
10 ml/2 tsp clear honey
5 ml/1 tsp lemon juice
2.5 ml/½ in piece of fresh root ginger, peeled and halved
1 whole clove
Plain yoghurt, to serve

1   Put all the ingredients in a bowl. Cover with pierced clingfilm
(plastic wrap) and leave to soak at room temperature for
2 hours.

2   Microwave on High for 3 minutes, stirring once during
cooking, until the fruit is tender and the remaining liquid thick
and syrupy.

3   Leave to stand for 2 minutes. Remove the ginger and clove
before serving either hot or at room temperature, with a little
plain yoghurt.

🕐 10 minutes plus soaking

Peanut Butter Cookies

Makes 14

50 g/2 oz/¼ cup soft light brown sugar
50 g/2 oz/¼ cup smooth peanut butter
15 g/½ oz/1 tbsp butter or margarine
1 egg, beaten
40 g/1½ oz/⅓ cup plain (all-purpose) flour
25 g/1 oz/¼ cup self-raising (self-rising) flour
A pinch of bicarbonate of soda (baking soda)
50 g/2 oz/½ cup salted peanuts, chopped

1   Beat together the sugar, peanut butter, butter or margarine and egg until well mixed.

2   Sift the flours and bicarbonate of soda over and stir into the mixture with the peanuts. Roll the mixture into 14 balls, then flatten slightly with the back of a fork (they'll spread during cooking).

3   Arrange seven of the biscuits around the edge of the turntable lined with baking parchment.

4   Microwave on Medium for 3 minutes until dry on the surface. Allow to cool for a few seconds, then remove and transfer to a wire rack to cool. Repeat with the remaining seven cookies.

🕐 *10 minutes*

Double Chocolate Chip Cookies

Makes 12

50 g/2 oz/¼ cup butter or margarine
50 g/2 oz/¼ cup soft light brown sugar
2.5 ml/½ tsp vanilla essence (extract)
75 g/3 oz/¾ cup self-raising (self-rising) flour
30 ml/2 tbsp cocoa (unsweetened chocolate) powder
25 g/1 oz/¼ cup chopped hazelnuts (filberts)
25 g/1 oz/¼ cup white chocolate drops
15 ml/1 tbsp milk

1 Cream the butter or margarine, sugar and vanilla essence until fluffy and light in colour. Sift the flour and cocoa powder over the mixture and mix in with the remaining ingredients.

2 Shape the mixture into 12 small balls and place six of them well apart around the edge of a flat plate lined with baking parchment. Flatten the cookies very slightly (they'll spread out during cooking).

3 Microwave on High for 1½ minutes or until the cookies are firm to the touch. Leave on the plate for 2 minutes, then transfer to a wire rack to cool. Repeat with the remaining six cookies.

🕑 10 minutes

Dark and Sticky Ginger Cake

Makes 8 slices

60 ml/4 tbsp golden (light corn) syrup
60 ml/4 tbsp black treacle (molasses)
75 g/3 oz/¾ cup soft dark brown sugar
100 g/4 oz/½ cup butter or margarine, plus extra for greasing
100 g/4 oz/1 cup self-raising (self-rising) flour
100 g /4 oz/1 cup wholemeal flour
5 ml/1 tsp ground ginger
5 ml/1 tsp mixed (apple-pie) spice
2.5 ml/½ tsp bicarbonate of soda (baking soda)
2 eggs, lightly beaten
Butter, for spreading (optional)

1 Put the syrup, black treacle, sugar and butter or margarine in a large bowl and microwave on Medium for 2 minutes or until the fat has melted, stirring halfway through cooking.

2 Sift the flours, ginger, mixed spice and bicarbonate of soda over, adding the bran left in the sieve (strainer). Add the eggs and mix together.

3 Pour the mixture into a lined and greased 1 kg/2 lb glass loaf dish and microwave on High for 4 minutes.

4 Allow to stand for 3–4 minutes before turning out and leaving to cool on a wire rack. When cold, cut into thick slices and serve buttered, if liked.

🕒 15 minutes

Index